Beading Beautiful Costume Jewelry

Patterns for Every Festive Occasion

Mary Ellen Harte

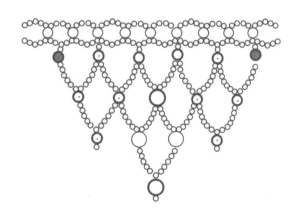

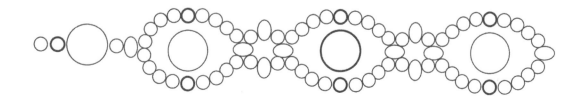

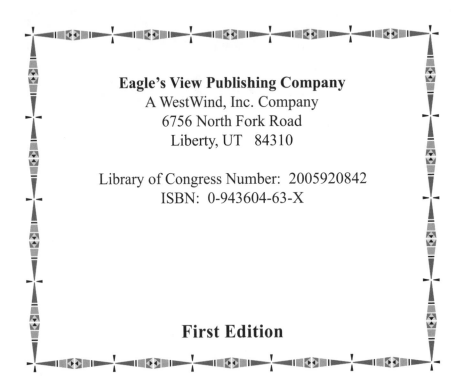

Eagle's View Publishing Company
A WestWind, Inc. Company
6756 North Fork Road
Liberty, UT   84310

Library of Congress Number: 2005920842
ISBN: 0-943604-63-X

First Edition

15 14 13 12 11 10 9 8 7 6 5 4 3 2 1

TABLE OF CONTENTS

DEDICATION

To my beloved daughter and husband,

Julia and John,

who continue to inspire & support me.

ABOUT THE AUTHOR

Mary Ellen ("Mel") Harte is a biologist, mother and craftsperson whose passion for pattern overflows into her other passions - beadwork, folk dancing and wildflowers. Her other productions include a CD wildflower guide to the Colorado Rockies, as well as CD photo albums of California native plants. An avid collector of ethnic textiles and crafts, she attempted to recreate a Native American beaded flower ring and pass the skill to her daughter. Deciphering existing bead patterns and creating her own, she eventually wrote *Simple Lace and Other Beaded Jewelry Patterns,* and later, *A Treasury of Beaded Jewelry*. This latest book bursts with beautiful patterns for festive occasions, from fun parties to formal balls. Mel migrates between Berkeley, CA and the Colorado Rockies. Periodically check out her website, www.beadwithmel.com, for new patterns. Photo taken by Michael Edison.

INTRODUCTION

Perhaps it's the Cinderella syndrome I caught when I was a child: I've always been fascinated by the sparkling jewelry of royalty - the diamonds flashing from Diana's tiara, the emeralds dripping from a Hollywood Queen's ears, and later on, the sapphires gleaming in the cases of the Louvre. It wasn't just their color or sparkle, I finally realized, but how those gems were arranged that produced such a dazzling effect. As interest in beadwork burgeoned in recent years, it became easy to buy an incredible array of sparkling glass beads in all shapes and sizes. This tempted me to re-create the "crown jewels" by creating beading patterns that mimic these faceted gems of fame, often using gold or silver seed beads as the setting against which larger, richly colored "gem" beads are displayed.

I offer you now my treasure trove, including an eclectic collection of designs that incorporate head pins, chains, non-faceted beads, and some fine lacy designs as well. By picking out your own color combinations you can create dazzling pieces that best match your wardrobe. But don't stop there - use this book as a springboard to create your own fancy jewelry designs. The sources of inspiration for designs are endless: magazine ads, pictures of models and Hollywood stars, books on costume jewelry, museum jewelry collections, estate sales, or as spontaneous as that woman at the party who passed by you wearing that gorgeous choker. After completing several projects in this book, try taking the next step: after admiring a particular jewelry piece of set gems, envision what that piece could look like as a beaded network, and you're on your way. The results of this book are elegant and glamorous, ready to be worn to a party, dance, celebration, ball or gala . . . or given as beautiful gifts!!

CHAPTER I: TOOLS AND TIPS OF THE TRADE

Even if you're eager to get started, read through this chapter before beginning a project. It talks about procedures that are considered a "given" in each project, and thus not mentioned in each project's description. It's also full of important tips on how to choose your tools and materials, use them, set up your workplace, and proceed with the beadwork. In order **to find color photos or instructions for each project,** from anywhere in the book, each set of instructions has a black and white photograph with the page number of its color photograph; each color photograph has the page number of the project instructions.

MATERIALS

Thread

I use **nylon beading thread, size E** (rarely F), and occasionally **Nymo size 0 thread,** depending on the project. **For any project, assume the use of size E thread, unless stated otherwise.** Nylon filament eventually degrades and breaks; any project I created with it more than 5 years ago and use frequently I have had to re-thread. Usually, the bigger the beads, the heavier the thread used, but the other limit is the number of times the thread can pass through the smallest bead opening, which becomes a crucial factor in some designs. If a project will be much heavier due to the use of much larger beads than those suggested here, and it has an elaborate network that demands passing the thread more than 4 times through some seed beads, consider using larger seed beads. Or use **Kevlar** thread, a very strong but relatively fine thread used in making such durable items as kayaks. My big, beautiful beaded collar from Russia, made of 6mm faceted beads, does not weigh more than 7 ounces but after having been worn only a few times the beaded network started to pull apart near the neckline as the weight of lower hanging beads stressed the fine thread used to create it. I was able to save the piece by reinforcing the neckline and the damaged area with Kevlar thread.

When threading very heavy beads, as in the Modern Art necklace, use **Beadalon© or Soft Flex©**, types of plastic coated steel wire cord that are made of several bundles of smaller threads twisted together. This thread is flexible, non-stretchable, and most importantly durable, unlike the superficially similar tigertail thread. Secure Beadalon© or Soft Flex© at the ends with crushable **crimp beads**.

Beads

I have purposely chosen beads of standard size and shape that are easily available from bead shops and catalogues, but I encourage the incorporation of your own unique beads into these patterns. **In the materials section of each project, overestimates of the number of needed beads are given**, rounding up to the nearest 10 or 100, except where only a few are needed. I use primarily **11/° colored transparent, gold or silver seed beads; delica** seed beads are more uniform and preferred. To find gold and silver beads, look for silver-lined topaz (gold) or silver-lined crystal (silver), which is how they are described online and in bead catalogues. This description refers to the silver-lined core that gives them their sparkling appearance. I also use fancier beads: those with iridescent, luster or rainbow (aurora borealis) finishes, or with cores differently colored from the rest of the bead (lined), for example. Various projects throughout this book, however, occasionally include seed beads ranging in size from **6/°** to **10/°**. The size refers to the number of beads that make up one inch, not when strung, but when laid down flat, end to end like a line of donuts. Individual beads vary both in the diameter of the hole and the bead itself. When a seed bead will require at least 4 passes of thread through it, search for a bead with a large hole and check that the thread fits through as many times as required before incorporating it into the piece. Think about using slightly larger seed beads, if the ones you have do not pass this simple test.

The larger "gem" beads are Czech glass, although using the more expensive Austrian Swarovski crystal will significantly increase the flash and sparkle of a piece. These larger glass beads include **7 or 8mm smooth or faceted transparent teardrops** (often simply referred to as drops), and **4, 6 or 8mm faceted transparent round** beads. I also use graduated (8 to 10mm) Chinese faceted teardrops. For any bead, a stated "color" varies in shade according to supplier and even batch to batch (see The Emerald City Necklace, for example), so make sure at the beginning that you have enough uniform beads for the planned piece.

Needles, Tools and Findings

Use a needle that fits through the smallest bead in a piece, and the smallest needle that will fit the thread being used. Consider cutting off or blunting the end of the needle to prevent it from piercing an already existing thread when sending the needle through a bead multiple times. When threading projects that use mostly large beads and require few passes through a single bead, use a **"Big Eye" beading needle**, which has an eye that extends for most of its length, making it easier to thread. For smaller beads, use a **size 10 beading needle,** but needle sizes are not standardized, so explore to see what works best. To make a flexible fine beading needle, fold the middle of a 5-inch piece of 34 gauge brass or silver colored wire (available in craft stores on spools) over a small nail to create the eye, then twist the two lengths together several times to form a fine, twisted shaft, trimming the ends with cutting pliers. Flag the working ends of thread with **narrow masking tape**, and snip excess thread with **fine, sharp scissors**. Use a white cotton or linen (not terry cloth) **dishtowel on a dinner tray** as a work surface; the beads don't roll and the work area is portable. Use **a grooved metal ruler** (one that detaches from a carpenter's square, available at hardware stores) to lay out strings of seed beads for easy threading.

Use **jump rings, spring clasps, head pins and earring findings** that can be held and manipulated easily to attach to finished pieces with 2 pairs of pliers: **serrated flat nosed pliers** and a **serrated rosary with cutter**. This latter pair is a round nosed pliers with a wire cutter, and can be used to make findings, such as a **simple S clasp**, quickly and cheaply, especially when working with sterling silver. For the clasp, clip off a 2-inch piece of 20 gauge surgical steel wire, and use the pliers to bend it into a vertically elongate "S," leaving a 1/8-inch gap between one end and the stem of the S. Hook the other end of the S through the loop of a piece and close that end. I often finish the ends as small loops so that no sharp end protrudes.

To make a **jump ring**, wrap 20-gauge sterling silver wire once completely around the cross section of the rosary pliers to create the desired size of jump ring. Remove the molded wire, and cut with the cutter. To reduce stress from the pull of other findings on the junction of the ring, attach the ring to the piece and gently compress the ring into an oval with the serrated flat nosed pliers, so that the junction occurs midway

An oval jump ring

along one side of the oval. When the piece is worn, the junction of the ring will never be stressed from contact with an adjacent jump ring or finding, which will hang from the extremities of the oval.

METHODS

Start with the simpler designs first. Examine the diagrams carefully. Once opened, **the book can be made to stay open on the table** by gently pressing the pages down and apart along the spine. The threaded diagrams are designed to be understood without the text. Just follow the arrows, tracing them with a pencil first if the pathway seems convoluted. Dashed lines usually indicate a section that is being rethreaded, often to get to the next part of the piece. To keep the threading pattern easy to follow in more complex designs, a series of diagrams are used to present successive threading sequences; an arrow indicates where identical subsequent patterns should be threaded. A dotted line often starts at the end of a series of identical patterns and turns into a solid line showing how a new section is to be threaded.

Think, and layout the design by placing beads on the pattern diagrams provided, if necessary. If unsure about how it will turn out, **test the design** with a short sequence. The lengths of the necklaces made in this book might not fit the intended neck, so be prepared to adjust that by adding more neckline pattern to either side of the necklace, and figure this into the bead budget. Alternatively, an extending chain can be added to the finished piece.

To start, **cut off 2-3 feet of thread** (for earrings 1-1.5 feet), **flag with masking tape 3 inches from one**

end, and remember to leave 3 inches at the end of the finished piece. The 3 inches allow thread to tie any necessary knots and to hide the remaining thread through existing beadwork. **Start most projects with a 5-8 seed bead loop** and re-thread the loop 2 or more times, keeping the loop taut. When the project is finished, connect an oval jump ring to this loop of beads and attach additional jump rings or clasps to the oval jump ring.

Avoid introducing unnecessary twists into the evolving beadwork by holding the piece continuously as more beads are added. **When the thread runs out**, choose an attachment place near big beads that can be used to hide the knot and thread ends. Cut a new length and attach it to the old length using 1-2 square knots. Leave 2-inch end threads for re-threading into the existing beadwork, but do not re-thread until the end of the project. This makes it easier to correct mistakes or make adjustments, and often the end of one thread is a good place to tie off the end of another thread originating from another part of the necklace.

Keep the work taut. To do so may require re-threading a section, either with the same thread, or a separate one, as the instructions suggest. When a group of hanging beads are connected to one bead (as in Rosy Veil), place all the beads flat, and adjust the tautness of the connecting threads so that the hanging part hangs straight down, before proceeding to the next part of the beadwork. If a finished piece twists too easily, or groups of small beads rotate around larger ones, the work isn't taut enough; re-thread it, especially through the rotating parts. If the rotation problem still persists, use clear nail polish to glue the strand of smaller beads to the larger one in the desired position. At the end of the project, go back and weave the thread ends through existing beadwork, using them to pull knots into big beads, and then cut off any exposed ends. When finished, **seal all knots with a dab of clear nail polish**.

Unless specified otherwise, **end necklaces with two linked jump rings** attached to one end loop, and **a jump ring linked to a spring clasp** attached at the other end. The extra jump rings add important flexibility to the end connections, where twisting occurs most often. This prevents the beadwork itself from awkward twisting. For the same reason, **add a jump ring to a finished earring, and link that, in turn, to an earring finding**. Add another jump ring if the earring doesn't hang at rest in the desired position.

Lastly, there is **the nightmare**: you are happily viewing the project you just finished when you see **a mistake** - smack in the middle of the piece. OK, so cry a bit. Then take the scissors and snip it open, pull off enough beads to expose a few inches on either end, attach some new thread, fix the offending section, tie the knots and hide the threads. Does this happen to me, and does the remedy really work? Yes, and yes.

Happy Beading !

CHAPTER II: NECKLACES

This section, using a diverse array of patterns, illustrates an evolution in the complexity of necklace designs. As the first project shows, creating even a single beautiful strand of beads requires careful thought but is worth the effort. The next step of complexity is to bind several single strands in parallel, and further, twist them to create a twisted rope (Kaleidoscope Choker). A single strand necklace becomes more intricate by simply adding modified "beads": beads strung on an earring wire that is added to the strand (Millennium), or threading hanging strands from the neckline (Rosy Veil). An interesting twist on the single strand necklace is created by connecting two parallel metal chains with beaded wires (Byzantine).

Another level in complexity occurs when the strand **circles** back on itself. This is done by sending the thread through one or more previously threaded beads *in the same direction as the original thread*. Circles are connected in sequence by one bead (**chain** sequence) or more than one bead (**ladder** sequence). The circles can be equal and overlapping (Crimson Crescent), interconnected and equal (Glittering Choker), or unequal (Rosebud). Further, the circles themselves can be modified, sometimes quite elaborately (Blossom, Emerald City, Eugenie's and Neapolitan). A network is created by connecting circles in a chain or ladder, and then connecting 2 or more chains or ladders running parallel to each other (Victorian); here, the circles are connected to each other from 3 or 4 sides (before, after, above and/or below). A tube necklace is made by connecting the first and last sequence of 3 or more parallel circle sequences.

Similarly, the same course in complexity is pursued by creating **loops**. This is done by sending the thread through a previously threaded bead *in the opposite direction of the original thread – i.e., through the same side of the bead from which the original thread emerges*. Although simple loops can be gussied up with complex sequences of interesting beads, much more interesting effects are achieved by elaborating the design of the loop itself, and interconnecting them to create elaborate networks of loops (Bridesmaid's Lace, Bridal Crystal, Elizabeth's, and Tiffany's) or by taking similar, simple loop sequences and connecting them in parallel (Dripping Diamonds).

True netting involves connecting sequences of loops or open **arches** (a sequence of beads suspended between two connecting points) in successively lower parallel layers (Blue Cascade) or adjacent parallel layers (Regal Bracelet). Connecting the first layer of arches with the last to form a tube is a popular necklace design. Elaborate loops can also be easily added to chain or ladder sequences to create truly ornate necklaces (Eugenie's).

Finally, one can create complex layered necklaces, connecting sequences of both loops and circles in successive parallel layers (La Condessa, Ruby Beauty, Superb Sapphire, and Diva's Delight).

Some final notes: 1) although 2 necklaces are designated for bridal purposes, obviously any of the designs in this section can be made into beautiful bridal jewelry, using crystals and pearls; 2) bracelet designs can be lengthened (and some widened as well, by adding an identical, second, connecting design parallel to the first) to create necklaces and chokers; 3) tube necklaces can be made by using larger beads and creating longer sequences of the designs used in the A la Fabergé bracelet.

MODERN ART NECKLACE

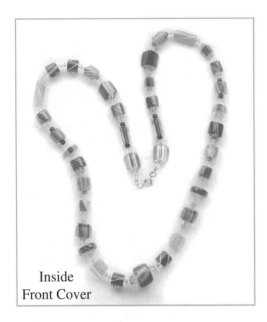

Inside
Front Cover

A simply strung strand of beads can be deceptively complex to sequence, and it was some time before I came up with an idea that properly shows off these American hand blown tube beads of various color combinations and geometric shapes. I have seen 20-inch necklaces of these priced at close to $200; you can make a longer one for about $30.

Use 49-strand Beadalon wire cord, not tigertail. Handpick the tube beads from the boxes at bead fairs or bead stores, where the beads are sold by the gram. For a 26-inch strand, get about 18 pairs of closely matching beads of various shapes and lengths, as well as a larger central one, if possible. I love bright rich colors, but go where the creative spirit leads you.

For each pair of beads, pick out 4 4mm round beads whose color complements those in the pair (e.g., garnet or opal blue with violet or red; crystal with yellow, blue and multicolors; turquoise or green with greens, black for dramatic effect); using clear crystal often will make the beads stand out and keep the necklace from becoming "too busy". If the bore hole engulfs 4mm beads, go to 6 or 8mm beads; or try crystal faceted beads, which are often a refreshing complement to the short tubes.

Layout your symmetrical sequence before stringing, mixing lengths, shapes and colors, but add some asymmetry to create a playful dimension. Start with a 30-inch length of Beadalon, loosely knotted. Add 2 crystal 4mm rounds. Add a tube & another crystal round; the rest are repeating patterns of: an 11/° crystal seed bead, a 4mm round, a tube bead, a 4mm round. End with 2 4mm crystal rounds.

Add a crimp bead, and loop the end through it until the loop is the size of a jump ring; crush the crimp flat with pliers, and trim the excess thread. Do the same to the other end, making sure the necklace is lying flat and the crimp is snug against the other beads before crushing. Add 2 jump rings to one end, and a jump ring & spring clasp to the other. Fini!

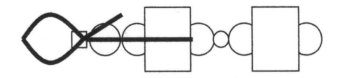

Materials:

36 pairs	4-6mm glass rounds, crystal & various colors
18 pairs	geometric glass blown tube beads, various lengths & colors
4	4-6mm crystal rounds
50	11/° crystal seed beads
30"	49 strand Beadalon thread
2	crimp beads

KALEIDOSCOPE NECKLACE/CHOKER

Inside
Front Cover

This is an incredibly easy and beautiful piece to assemble! Using size F thread, string 3 (emerald, amethyst and sapphire) strands of 51 8mm faceted round beads each, spaced by single 11/° gold seed beads between each 8mm bead, with triplets of gold beads at both ends. String an equally long strand (using size E thread) of freshwater pearls. Thread all 4 strands through a 6/° gold bead, and create a loop of 8/° gold seed beads, going out through the 6/° bead. Knot the thread ends and trim any excess. Connect the end loops to jump rings and a clasp. Twist the ropes 5-6 times before securing the clasp to create a twisted rope. Create different color combinations to suit your particular need.

Materials	250	11/° gold seed beads		Sizes E & F thread
	90	freshwater pearls	2	6/° gold seed beads
	51	8mm faceted round beads of each color: amethyst, emerald, sapphire		

Necklace twisted 6 times:

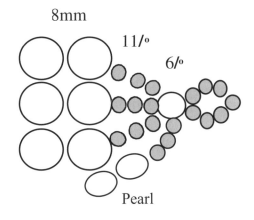

8mm
11/°
6/°
Pearl

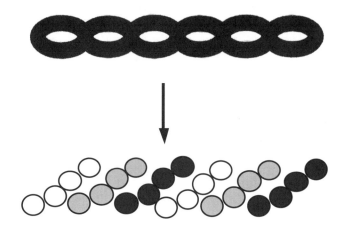

Variations: 1) String five 27-inch lengths from a mix of assorted seed beads (size 9/°-11/°, transparent, opaque, & tinsel of various colors) and variously colored #2 (4.5 mm) tinsel bugles, leaving 3 inches on either end. Use about 10 seed beads for every bugle bead. Line up the beads on the grooved ruler of a carpenter's square, and then scoop them up along the beading needle onto the thread. Bundle the 5 strands together at each end and make one knot of all the strand ends. Thread and knot a double length of cord, and thread this through the bundled knot. Thread through a snub nose bullet end bead, then through a slightly smaller bead (size 5/°) and then attach to a jump ring or S clasp. Re-thread through the size 5/° bead and through the bundled knot; knot the end, then trim and hide all threads.

You now have a nice necklace to wear. OR, close the necklace, and put a finger through the loop of strands at the clasp. Twist the necklace loop 6 times from the other end. The various strands will form a thick

KALEIDOSCOPE NECKLACE/CHOKER (cont.)

twisted rope of beads - connect the little loop at both ends with a bead ring (available at costume jewelry shops) or a large S clasp, and wear a really classy thick beaded choker!!

2) Make 14+ inch lengths to create thick beaded rope bracelets.

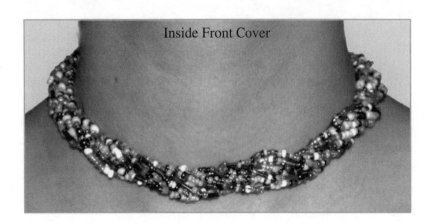

Inside Front Cover

THE   MILLENNIUM   NECKLACE (cont.)

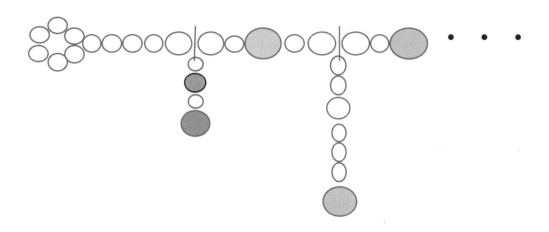

THE MILLENNIUM NECKLACE

So named by a friend who was reminded of the 2000 fireworks upon seeing it, this 14-inch necklace is made of 19 beaded head pins, strung along a beaded neckline. The head pins have 4 and 6mm faceted rounds of various colors, interspersed with 11/° gold beads. Make the beaded head pins first, then thread them on the neckline. The bead sequences of the first 9 and the 10th central head pins are shown below; reverse the order of the first 9 head pins for the second half of the necklace. The repeating neckline sequence (after the loop & 4 gold seed

Page 17

beads) is: a head pin between two 4mm crystal faceted rounds, then a gold seed bead, a 6mm faceted round, and a gold seed bead. The color sequence of the 6mm neckline beads are: light yellow, light green, amethyst, ruby, green, sapphire blue, olivine, amethyst, light yellow; this sequence is reversed for the second half of the neckline (as in the Modern Art Necklace, the sample piece has some asymmetry added). Once you've threaded the neckline, re-thread back to the beginning and pull taut; knot the 2 ends.

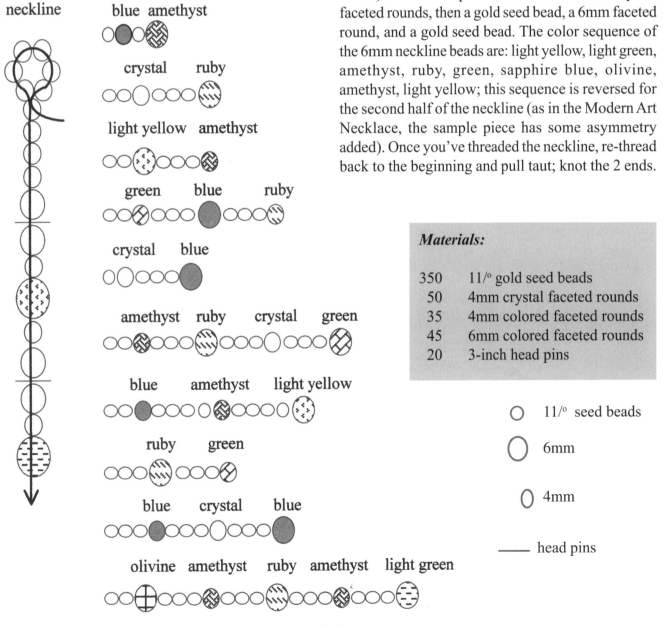

Materials:

350	11/° gold seed beads
50	4mm crystal faceted rounds
35	4mm colored faceted rounds
45	6mm colored faceted rounds
20	3-inch head pins

○   11/° seed beads

◯   6mm

○   4mm

—— head pins

13

ROSY VEIL NECKLACE

Page 17

This necklace uses the same basic pattern as the Millennium Necklace, but the use of graduated threaded hanging strands of beads creates a very different effect. After the 4 bead loop, thread the neckline with a repeating sequence of pearl seed bead, 2 gold seed beads, 1 6mm bead and 2 gold seed beads (19 6mm beads total), then double back and add the hanging threads. Lay each just-finished thread out flat and center the tautness of the thread on both sides of the connecting neckline bead so that the strand hangs straight, not asymmetrically. There will be 15 strands, increasing from one to eight 8mm faceted round rose beads in length then decreasing backing to one again. The neckline pattern and first 5 strands are shown; follow it for the rest of the strands. *Variations*: substitute 4mm beads for all the hanging 6mm beads except the terminal ones; make the terminal beads a different color from those of the hanging strands.

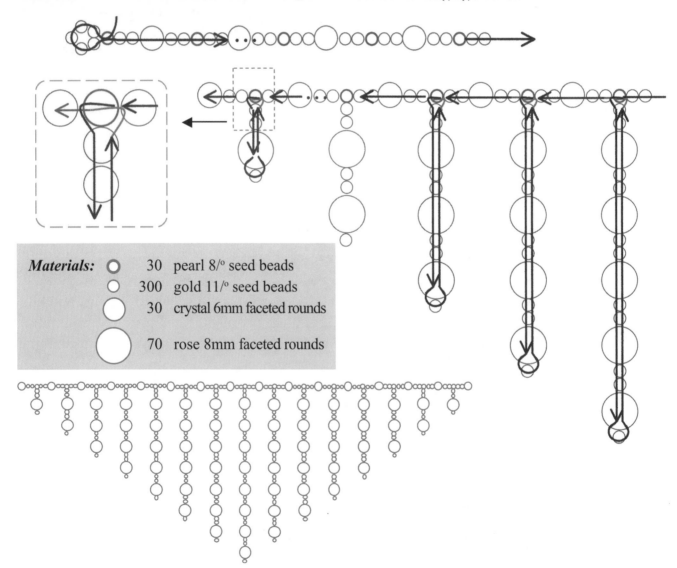

Materials:

○	30	pearl 8/° seed beads
○	300	gold 11/° seed beads
○	30	crystal 6mm faceted rounds
○	70	rose 8mm faceted rounds

RAJAH PEARL NECKLACE

Sometimes the simplest necklace can look so pretty, and so it is with this pattern, whether done with just gold seed beads or faceted garnets. Start the neckline with a loop, then do 14 sequences of a 4mm pearl and 13 gold seed beads; end with a pearl and another loop. Re-thread back an inch or so to the next-to-last pearl. From there, thread the 12 triangles, each consisting of 12 gold seed beads on a side and a bottom dangle of a gold seed bead, a big pearl, a crystal and another gold seed bead. Re-thread through the last neckline segment at the end, and knot with the beginning of the thread.

Page 18

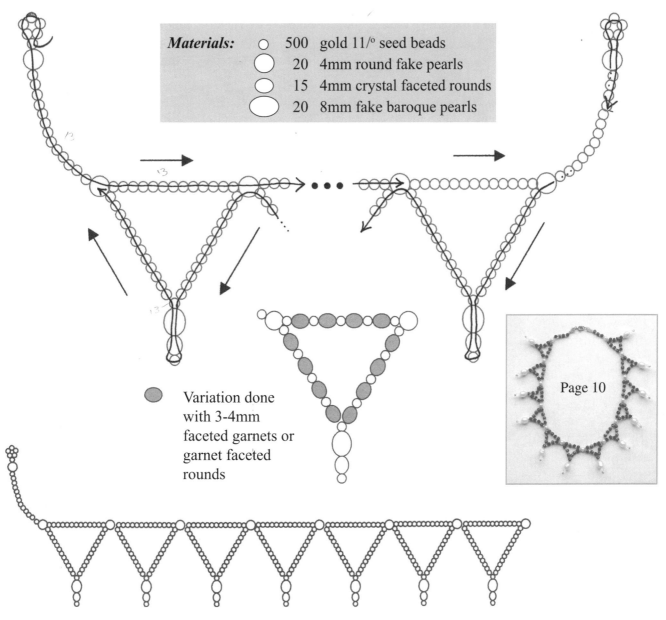

Materials:
- ○ 500 gold 11/° seed beads
- ○ 20 4mm round fake pearls
- ○ 15 4mm crystal faceted rounds
- ○ 20 8mm fake baroque pearls

● Variation done with 3-4mm faceted garnets or garnet faceted rounds

Page 10

15

BYZANTINE NECKLACE

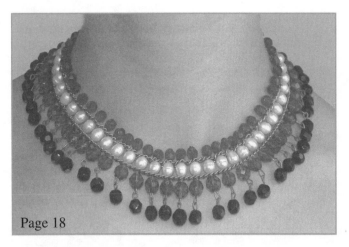

Page 18

I copied this Byzantine design from an antique necklace mistakenly offered for sale at a yard sale. Fold a 29-inch chain into a double, untwisted 14.5-inch length; link the free ends with a jump ring. Thread a 6mm faceted round red crystal bead onto a 2-inch head pin; this smaller, 6mm top bead prevents "top-heavy" twisting of the necklace when worn. Use the thickest head pin that will fit through the hole of the pearls. Starting 1 inch from the doubled end of the chain, insert the inverted earring pin through a single link of the upper chain. Add a freshwater pearl, then insert the head pin through a single link of the lower chain, also 1 inch from the end, so that no twist occurs in the entire chain. Add an 8mm faceted round smoke crystal bead, then snip off all but 1/3 inch of the remaining pin length; curve the remaining head pin end with the pliers into a closed hook. Similarly, add 41 more head pins, spacing each by 3 links, keeping the chains free of twists.

Put a 7mm faceted round jet bead on a 1-inch head pin, snip all but 1/3 inch of the remaining unbeaded pin length, and curve the remainder into a hook. Hook this onto the closed hooked end of the beaded head pin attached to the doubled chain, and close the hook. Repeat 41 more times. Attach 2-3 inches of chain to the doubled end with a jump ring, add a jump ring at the free end, and a spring clasp to the other end. Make matching earrings. Voila!

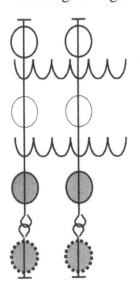

6mm round faceted red crystal beads

chain links

8mm freshwater pearls

chain links

8mm round faceted smoke crystal beads

7mm faceted jet beads

Materials:

42	6mm red crystal faceted round
42	1-inch head pins
42	8mm freshwater pearls
42	2-inch head pins
42	8mm 8 topaz faceted rounds
42	7mm jet black faceted rounds
35	inches gold plate curb chain, 10 links per inch

Matching earring:

4mm faceted red

8/o pearl

7mm faceted jet black

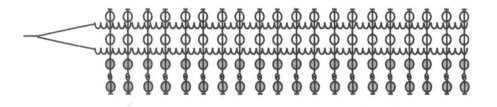

16

Page 13

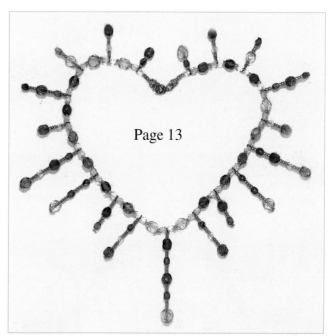

Page 13

Page 14

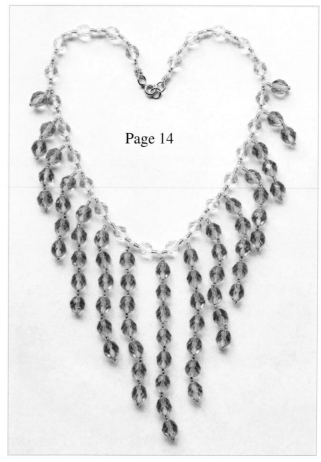

Page 14

Page 15

Page 15

Page 15

Page 16

Page 16

Page 21

Page 21

Page 22

Page 22

Page 23

Page 23

Page 24

Page 24

Page 25

Page 25

CRIMSON CRESCENT NECKLACE

This simple and elegant 13.5-inch necklace consists of 6 overlapping crescents. Create a neckline using the pattern below, beginning & ending as shown, and using 20 ruby 4mm faceted round beads. The sequence between ruby beads is one garnet seed bead, 2 crystal seed beads, a 3mm crystal faceted round, 2 crystal seed beads and a garnet seed bead. Attach a second thread to the beginning of the first and re-thread through

Page 19

the neckline to just before the 4th ruby bead, then add the sequence of crescent beads shown below (3 gold and 1 garnet seed bead, 1 4mm ruby bead, 1 garnet, 3 gold and 1 garnet seed, 1 6mm ruby bead, 1 garnet, 3 gold and 1 garnet seed, 1 6mm ruby bead, 1 garnet, 3 gold, and 1 garnet seed bead, 1 8mm ruby bead, and 1 garnet seed bead, followed by 24 crystal seed beads on the right half). *Skip 4 ruby neckline beads and attach the crescent just after the 4th one, sending the thread *back* through it and the next one. At that point, add another crescent sequence that overlaps the previous one and repeat from *. When you attach the 6th crescent, send the thread *forward* through the neckline, and knot with the end of the first thread.

Materials:				
◑	200	gold 11/° seed beads	◯ 26	ruby 4mm faceted rounds
●	100	garnet 11/° seed beads	◯ 6	ruby 6mm faceted rounds
◯	150	crystal 11/° seed beads	◯ 19	crystal 3mm faceted rounds
◯	6	ruby 8mm faceted rounds		

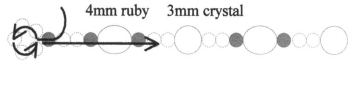

4mm ruby   3mm crystal

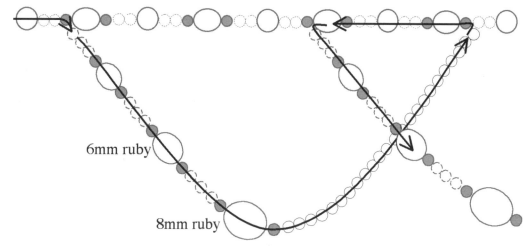

6mm ruby

8mm ruby

21

ALEXANDRA'S GALA NECKLACE

Page 19

Evocative of old Russian aristocracy, this seemingly elaborate 16-inch necklace is actually a variation on a simple lace loop chain. Create a dangle (to go through a loop closure) with an amethyst 8mm faceted round, then start the lace loop as shown. Make 23 diamond motifs; the 4th, 8th, 12th, and 16th ones will be light sapphire, and the rest will be amethyst. The beads between the diamonds are gold. End with a loop (about 17 beads) through which the dangle on the opposite end will fit snugly.

Materials:	○	600	gold 11/° seed beads	
	○	300	metallic purple iris 11/° seed beads	
	◔	100	light blue silver-lined 11/° seed beads	
	○	25	crystal 4mm faceted rounds	

○	100	amethyst 4mm faceted rounds
◔	20	lt sapphire 4mm faceted rounds
◯	1	amethyst 8mm faceted round

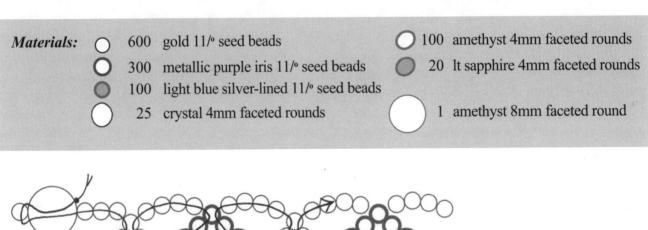

Opposite end

Light sapphire
diamond pattern

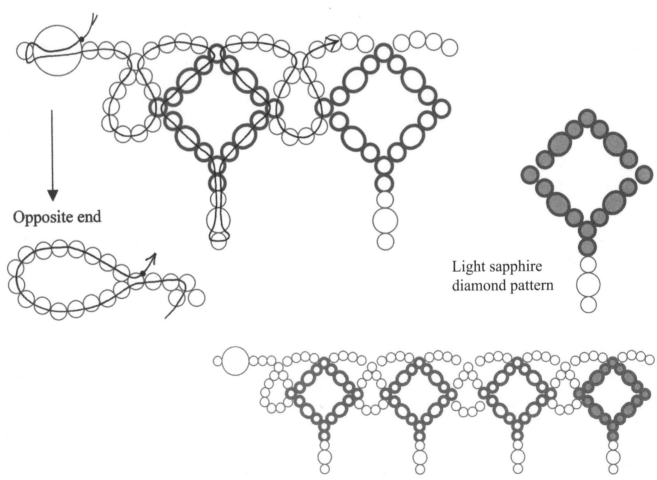

22

ROSEBUD NECKLACE

This 14-inch Victorian style necklace has an upper strand of beads interspersed with 5 floral patterns. Start a neckline with a loop and two seed beads, then 4 of the 4mm rounds, each separated by a triplet of a purple, a fuchsia and a purple bead (**a**). Make 5 rosebuds using 8mm rounds, seed beads and a central pearl bead as shown (4 of **b** and one central **c**), separating them by segments of 6 4mm rounds interspersed with the same purple-fuchsia seed bead triplets as in the beginning; the rosebud segments begin and end with a gold and a purple bead. The third, central rosebud (**c**) contains 5 8mm rounds and the hanging drop is added later.

Page 19

Starting at the first rosebud, add a second, lower line (dashed, **d**) of connecting looping segments, also adding the drop hanging from the central rosebud. The first and last looping segment have 8 4mm rounds with the seed bead triplets; the two middle looping segments have 10 4mm rounds. In each looping segment, the fuchsia bead of the centermost bead triplet should be replaced by a gold seed bead, giving added sparkle to the piece.

Materials:	200	gold 11/° seed beads		200	iridescent fuchsia 11/° seed beads
	200	iridescent purple 11/° seed beads		1	garnet 4mm faceted round
	5	white pearl 8/° seed beads		1	amethyst 10mm faceted drop
	70	topaz luster 4mm faceted rounds		25	amethyst 8mm faceted rounds

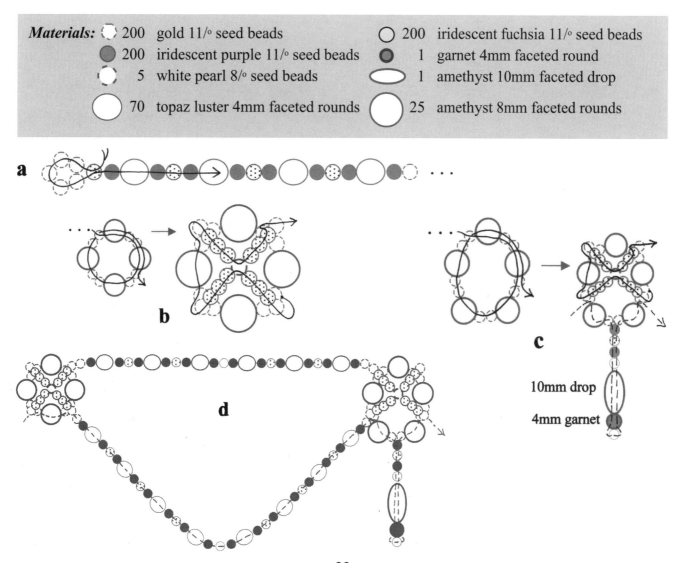

23

PEARLS & PERIWINKLES NECKLACE

Page 20

Elegance with ease characterizes this 14.5 inch necklace. Start the neckline with a gold loop, then 2 aurora borealis (AB) finish amethyst 4mm faceted rounds, then 34 amethyst 8mm faceted rounds, with a gold 11/° seed bead between all of the faceted beads. End the neckline as it was started, with a loop. Re-thread back to the beginning 4mm AB amethyst bead and knot, but do not cut the thread. Reverse and go back through the neckline with the remaining thread, exiting at the first 8mm amethyst bead. Start adding the overlaying circles: add 6 AB amethyst 4mm faceted rounds, then send the thread back through the neckline starting at the second 4mm bead and exiting from the second 8mm bead. Add 5 3-4mm pearls, then 8 crystal 11/° seed beads and circle back, sending the thread back through the neckline from the first amethyst 8mm bead through the third 8mm bead. Create the next circle: add 4 4mm AB amethysts, then 8 crystal seeds, circling the thread back through the second to fourth neckline 8mm beads. Alternate pearl with amethyst circles, creating 34 circles in all. Each new circle will *underlap* the previous circle. The last circle contains pearls.

Materials: ○ 70 gold 11/° seed beads   ○ 300 crystal 11/° seed beads

○ 100 3-4mm pearls   ○ ○ 80 amethyst AB 4mm faceted rounds

○ 40 amethyst 8mm faceted rounds

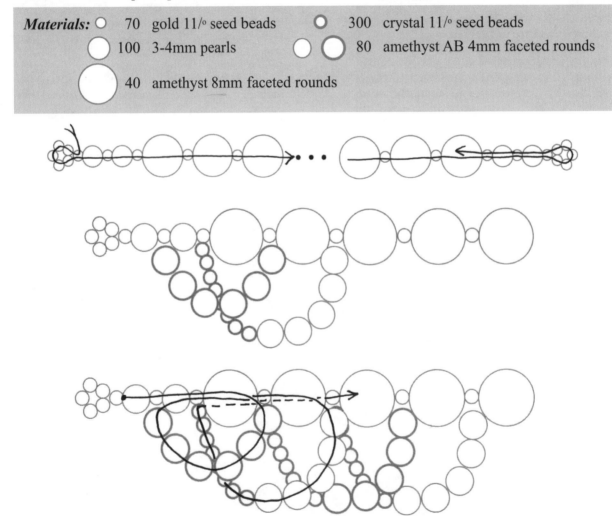

24

GLITTERING CHOKER

Perfect for the New Year's Eve Party!! This 14.5 inch elaborate variation of a ladder pattern has garnet (G) or red (R) x-shaped flowers that alternate with 4-petal circle flowers of milky white (W). Start and end with a loop of 1 gold bugle and 10 gold seed beads. The flower sequence is: GWGW**R**W, G, W**R**WGWG. Use black nylon beading thread, size E; this project is easier with a big eye needle. Re-thread through the loops that create the x-shaped flowers in the piece (re-threading not shown below), as they are made.

Page 20

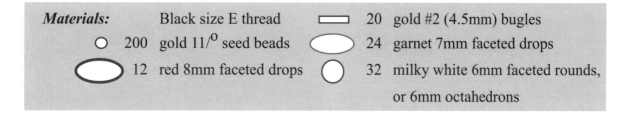

Materials:		Black size E thread		20	gold #2 (4.5mm) bugles
○	200	gold 11/^{o} seed beads		24	garnet 7mm faceted drops
	12	red 8mm faceted drops		32	milky white 6mm faceted rounds, or 6mm octahedrons

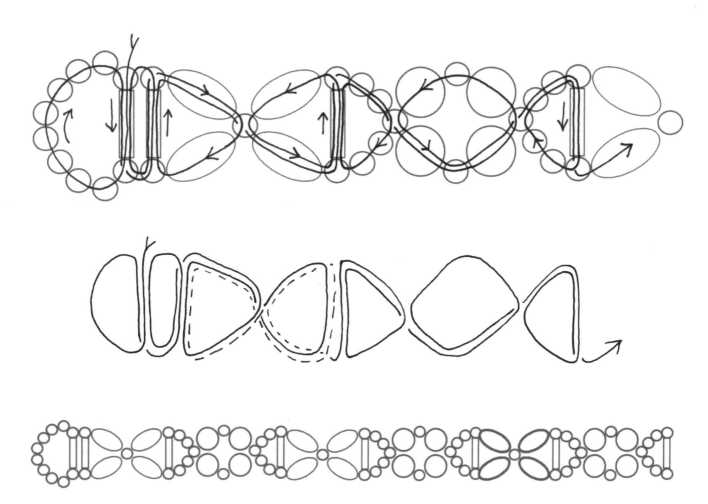

25

BLOSSOM NECKLACE

Page 37

This 13.5 inch necklace illustrates how to make jeweled blossoms. Start with a loop and thread the sequence below (a-c) then add the overlay onto the "blossom" (d-e), and repeat the single sequence of a-c backwards to finish. The bead in the center of the blossom is an amethyst 4mm faceted round. Variation: make a choker or bracelet of linked blossoms!

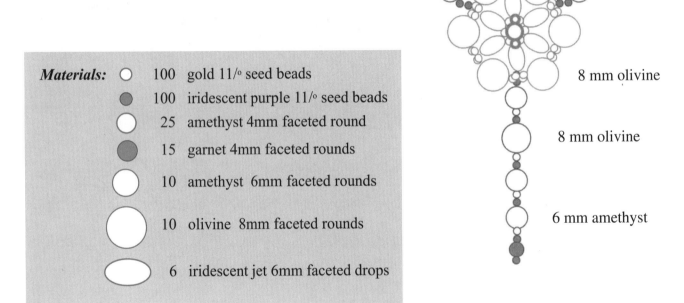

6 mm amethyst

8 mm olivine

8 mm olivine

8 mm olivine

6 mm amethyst

Materials:

○	100	gold 11/° seed beads
●	100	iridescent purple 11/° seed beads
○	25	amethyst 4mm faceted round
●	15	garnet 4mm faceted rounds
○	10	amethyst 6mm faceted rounds
○	10	olivine 8mm faceted rounds
○	6	iridescent jet 6mm faceted drops

a

b

26

BLOSSOM NECKLACE

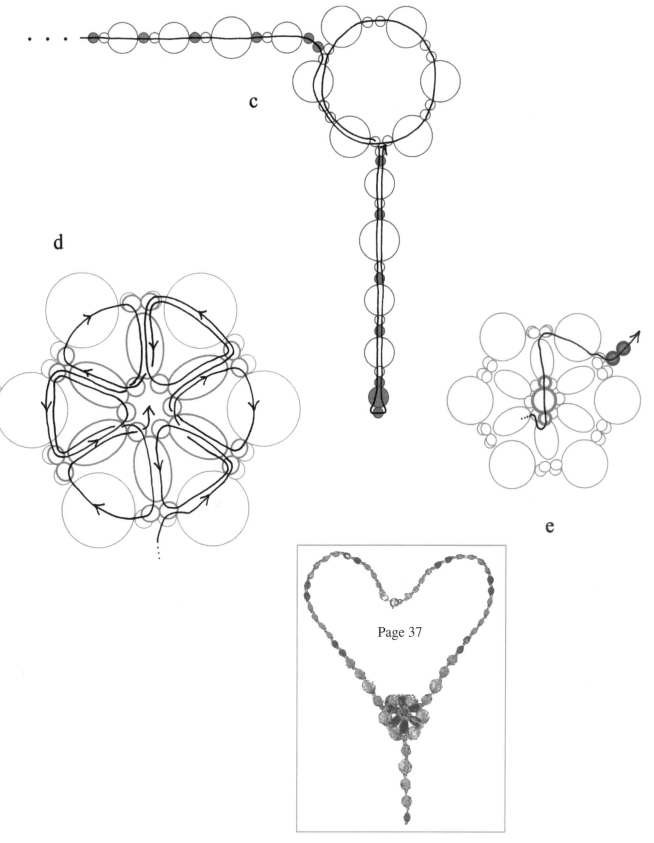

c

d

e

Page 37

EUGENIE'S NECKLACE

Page 37

Fit for Napoleon's consort, this 14.5-inch sapphire blue necklace is a complex chain that links 8 modified Empress earrings together. Make a loop of gold and pearl seed beads, then thread on the first **a** pattern (crystal 4mm and gold seed beads) and pull taut; knot with the end tail of the thread. Re-thread (dashed line in diagram) through the first bead past the knot. Go outside the anchor bead of the end loop and re-thread back through the anchor bead; re-thread through **a** to start **b.** End the piece similarly. In all, do 8 **abac** patterns, ending with **aba**. The **b** pattern is a circle of light sapphire 4mm and gold seed beads with pearl seed beads and a center 3mm sapphire bead added after the dangle. The **c** pattern has cobalt 4mm beads interspersed with gold seed beads and a central sapphire 4mm round. All beads except seed beads are faceted rounds.

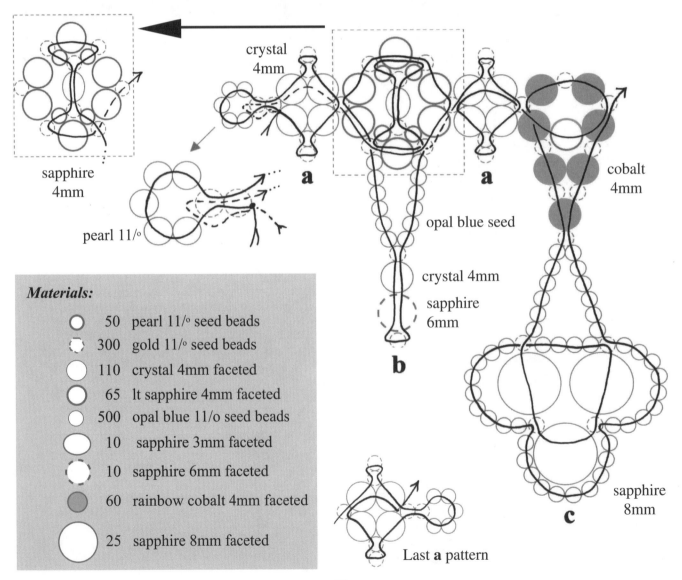

crystal
4mm

sapphire
4mm

pearl 11/°

a

a

opal blue seed

crystal 4mm

sapphire
6mm

b

cobalt
4mm

sapphire
8mm

c

Last **a** pattern

Materials:

○	50	pearl 11/° seed beads
⬡	300	gold 11/° seed beads
○	110	crystal 4mm faceted
○	65	lt sapphire 4mm faceted
○	500	opal blue 11/o seed beads
○	10	sapphire 3mm faceted
⬭	10	sapphire 6mm faceted
●	60	rainbow cobalt 4mm faceted
○	25	sapphire 8mm faceted

28

NEAPOLITAN CHOKER

This 13-inch overlain ladder choker is based on one I bought from a street vendor in Naples; many were selling variations of either overlain or multi-ladder chokers, all in black (their large beads were rondelles). Note it is a ladder pattern, overlain with a second ladder pattern. Start with a simple chain pattern **a**, using 7 sapphire blue 6mm faceted rounds for each sequence (the 7ᵗʰ is at the beginning of **b**, below). Do 8 patterns of the more elaborate ladder shown in (**b**), making sure the holes of the gold 11/° beads are big enough to accept 3 widths of E beading thread and 4 widths of Nymo 0 thread. End with the **a** sequence of 7 blue 6mm rounds. Use Nymo 0 thread for the second thread to add the 7 overlying ladder patterns (**c**) to **b**, re-threading each overlying pattern when it is done, and keeping it all taut. The overlying pattern will crimp the underlying one a little, causing the 3 larger middle beads to pop outwards or inwards slightly, but this disappears with wear. Knot & hide threads. Si bella!

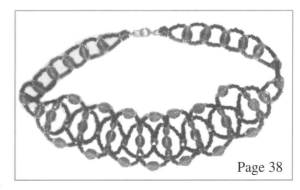

Page 38

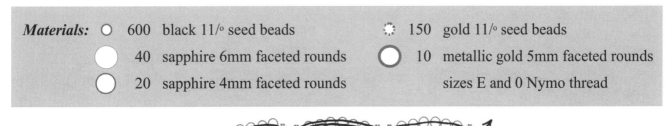

Materials: ○ 600 black 11/° seed beads   ✦ 150 gold 11/° seed beads

   ○   40 sapphire 6mm faceted rounds   ◎   10 metallic gold 5mm faceted rounds

   ○   20 sapphire 4mm faceted rounds   sizes E and 0 Nymo thread

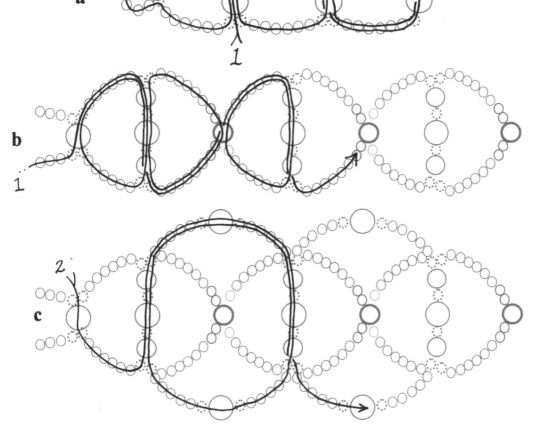

EMERALD CITY NECKLACE

Page 38

For beads, the color emerald green varies from almost watery green to deep blue green. As Dorothy searched for the Emerald City so I searched and eventually found the rich deep green in a discontinued batch of 8mm faceted rounds. This 15-inch necklace, patterned after a ruby necklace owned by Jackie Onassis, needs two threads: one (1) for the neckline ladder pattern (**I**), and a second (2) to attach added neckline beads and the dangles (**II**). The ladder pattern (see inset box) is 5 sequences of **abcb**: a quartet of 8mm, a quartet of 6mm, a sextet of 8mm with a cross lattice (and dangle), and a quartet of 6mm. End with a quartet of 8mm. The 2nd and 4th sextets have threading patterns inverted from that shown. The neckline pattern without the dangles makes a great choker.

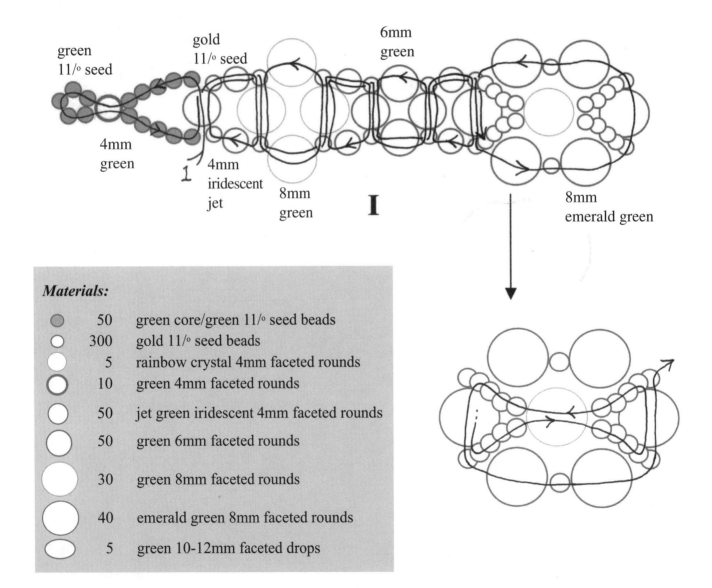

green
11/° seed

gold
11/° seed

6mm
green

4mm
green

1

4mm
iridescent
jet

8mm
green

I

8mm
emerald green

Materials:

⬤	50	green core/green 11/° seed beads
○	300	gold 11/° seed beads
○	5	rainbow crystal 4mm faceted rounds
○	10	green 4mm faceted rounds
○	50	jet green iridescent 4mm faceted rounds
○	50	green 6mm faceted rounds
○	30	green 8mm faceted rounds
○	40	emerald green 8mm faceted rounds
○	5	green 10-12mm faceted drops

EMERALD CITY NECKLACE

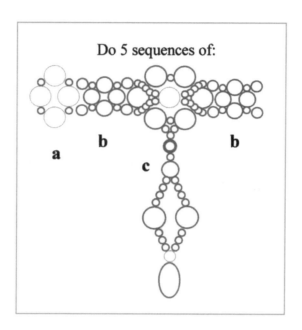

Do 5 sequences of:

a   b   b

c

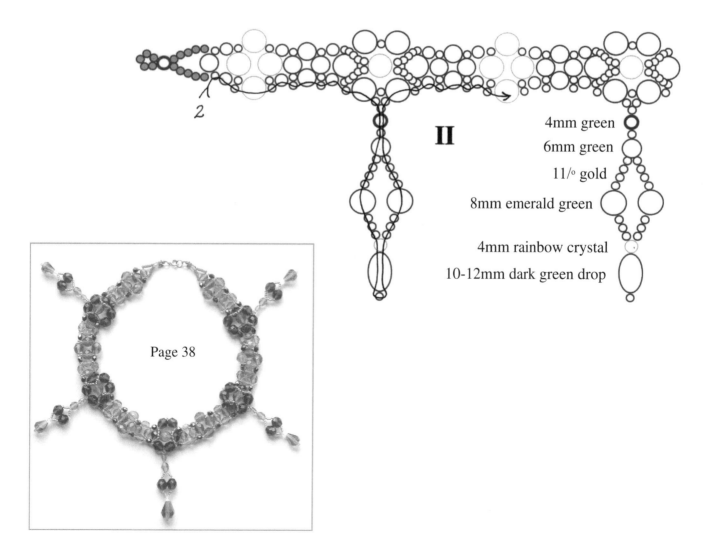

2

II

4mm green

6mm green

11/º gold

8mm emerald green

4mm rainbow crystal

10-12mm dark green drop

Page 38

VICTORIAN CHOKER

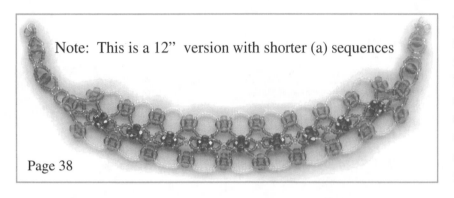

Note: This is a 12" version with shorter (a) sequences

Page 38

In this 14-inch choker 3 ladder sequences are connected and running in parallel to each other. Start with the lead sequence (**a**) of amethyst seed beads with gold seed accents around 3 single olivine 6mm rounds. Next do the more elaborate sequence (**b**) in the middle of the choker. It consists of 11 quartets of 4mm faceted rounds:
the 1st and 11th quartets are olivine, the others iridescent copper or jet. End with a second sequence (**a**). Start a second thread at the first quartet and add the lower chain of 10 olivine quartets, going right, to the end of the middle sequence (**b**). End the lower chain at the last olivine quartet and thread through it to start the upper chain, going left (**c**); re-thread to the beginning of the second thread and knot.

Materials:

○	400	amethyst 11/° seed beads	◌	300	gold 11/° seed beads
⬤	6	olivine 6mm faceted rounds	○	100	olivine 4mm faceted rounds
○	40	copper **or** metallic iridescent jet green 4mm faceted rounds	○	10	iridescent amethyst 11/° seed beads
			●	200	crystal 11/° seed beads

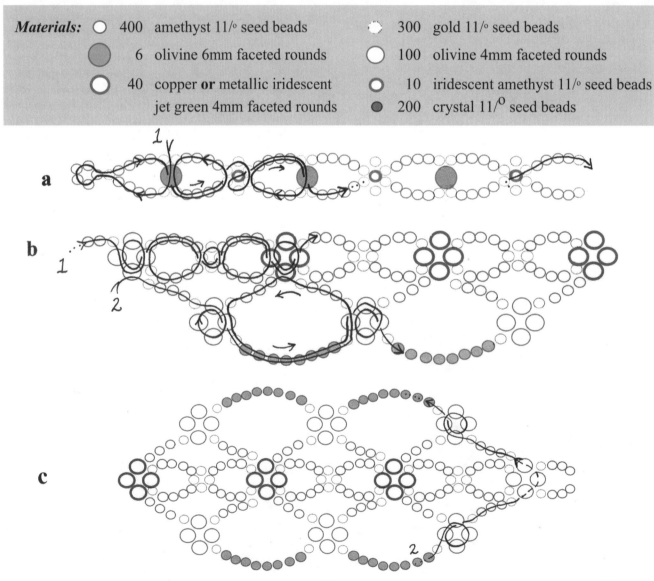

a

b

c

32

DRIPPING DIAMONDS NECKLACE

Although the original piece (pictured) is 12.5 inches long with 13 dripping diamond patterns, I suggest doing at least 15 patterns (about 14.5 inches long), so that the dripping diamonds surround your neck. This means adding 13 patterns to the two shown. The patterns consist of a quartet of olivine 6mm faceted rounds with gold seed beads interspersed and pearl seed beads at the top and bottom. The dangles have a gold seed, a 4mm sapphire round, a gold and a pearl seed, an 8 or 10mm faceted drop and a gold seed bead. There are 6mm sapphire rounds between the quartets, with pearl seeds on either side. The neckline consists of crystal seeds, with a gold seed above each pattern and a gold seed, lavender 4mm round, gold seed design centered between each of the olivine patterns. Thread the lower part first then attach the neckline, re-threading the neckline (dashed line) back to the beginning of the piece. It is equally elegant without drops!

Page 39

Materials:
○	200	crystal 11/° seed beads	200	gold 11/° seed beads
	70	olivine 6mm faceted rounds	20	sapphire 6mm faceted rounds
	20	sapphire 4mm faceted rounds	20	lavender luster 4mm faceted rounds
	20	lt sapphire 8-10mm faceted drops	80	pearl 8/° seed beads

← 13 more patterns here →

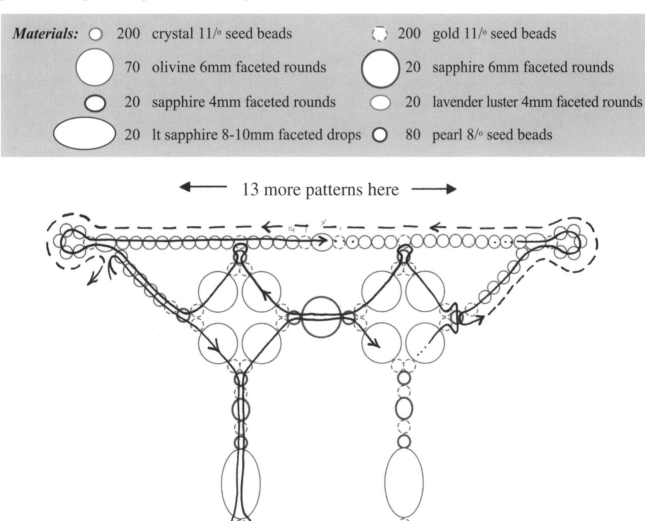

33

ELIZABETH'S NECKLACE

Page 39

The inspiration for these two 14-inch variations came from the necklace worn by the young yet-to-be Queen Elizabeth in the movie *Elizabeth*, and they evoke plenty of awe whenever I wear either version. The difference is either 6mm or 8mm drops at the bottom and how these are threaded. Because the threaded needle does not fit through the top of the cross-drilled 6mm teardrop beads, the needle must be rethreaded after every teardrop. Not so for the 8mm drops, where the thread goes through vertically. Thread the lower part first, then thread the top triplets of seed beads. Finally, using size 0 Nymo thread (dashed line), thread through the triplets and neckline, keeping it taut to tighten up the whole piece, and prevent the triplets from rotating; once finished, brush the backs of the triplets with clear nail polish. Make 32 patterns, and end as you began (shown in the first diagram).

Materials:

○	300	gold 11/° seed beads	● 100	purple iridescent 11/° seed beads
○	40	matte green 6/° seed beads	○ 40	matte blue-green 6/° seed beads
○	40	milky green 6mm smooth drops	○ 80	green/turquoise core 6/° seed beads
⬭	**OR** 40	milky green 8mm smooth drops		

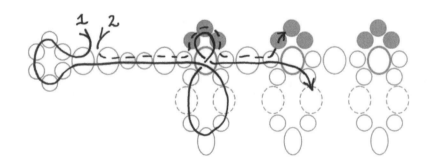

34

ELIZABETH'S NECKLACE

Page 39

Page 39

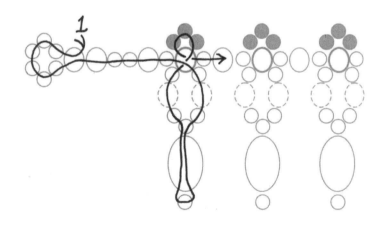

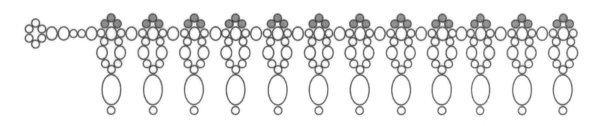

BRIDESMAID'S LACE NECKLACE

Page 40

This is a nice complement to the Bridal Necklace that can be worn by the bridesmaids. This 15-inch necklace requires 15 *fleur de lis* patterns. It is important to keep the beadwork taut when looping on and re-threading the single beads. Remember to re-thread through all looped beads (shaded), as indicated by the dashed lines in the magnified inset areas. Once the necklace is finished, brush the backs of these areas with nail polish to keep them from rotating. *Variation*: add a 6-8mm pink faceted drop bead to the lowest part of the *fleur de lis* pattern.

Materials: 1,000 peachy pink pearl 11/° seed beads

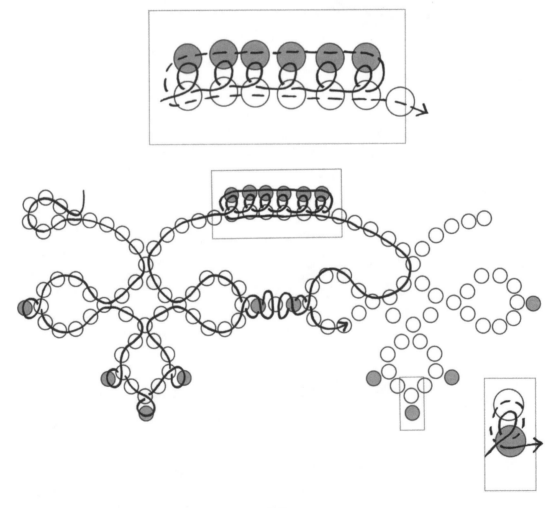

Page 26

Page 26

Page 28

Page 28

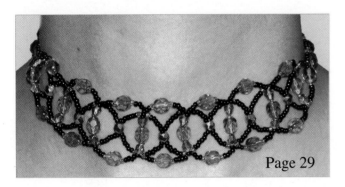

Page 29

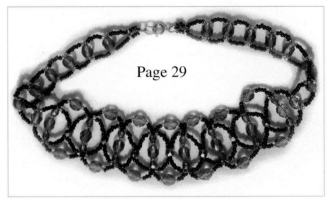

Page 29

Page 30

Page 30

Page 32

Page 32

Page 33

Page 33

Page 34

Page 34

Page 34

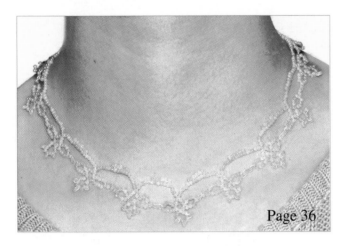

Page 36

Page 36

Page 41

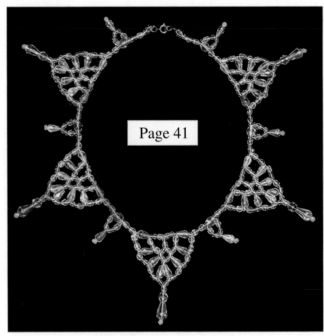

Page 41

40

BRIDAL CRYSTAL NECKLACE

This 14-inch, two-strand necklace is for the bride who wants to go all out with a truly fancy, elaborate necklace. Start with a loop of crystal seeds and a 3mm round. Add the neckline 4mm rounds and crystal seeds and then one small drop pattern. The small drop starts with a 6mm round and has crystal seeds, 4mm rounds, 3mm rounds, a 7mm drop and an 8/° pearl seed. Add the neckline beads. Next, do a large drop pattern and a small one. Repeat this step 5 times, ending with an end loop. The large drop uses 3mm and 4mm rounds along with 7mm drops. The dangle has a 6mm round an 8mm drop, and an 8/° pearl seed. Re-thread the neckline to reinforce and shape the patterns. *Variations*: Substitute the dark rimmed 11/° crystal bead with a gold one. Make Empress Earrings to match. Splurge and use Swarovski crystals!

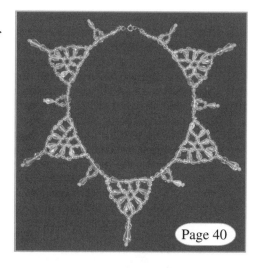

Page 40

Materials:

○ 100	crystal 3mm faceted rounds	○○ 200 crystal 11/° seed beads
○ 15	crystal 6mm faceted rounds	○ 120 crystal 4mm faceted rounds
◎ 15	pearl 8/° seed bead	◯ 50 rainbow crystal 7mm faceted drops
◯ 5	rainbow crystal 8mm faceted drops	

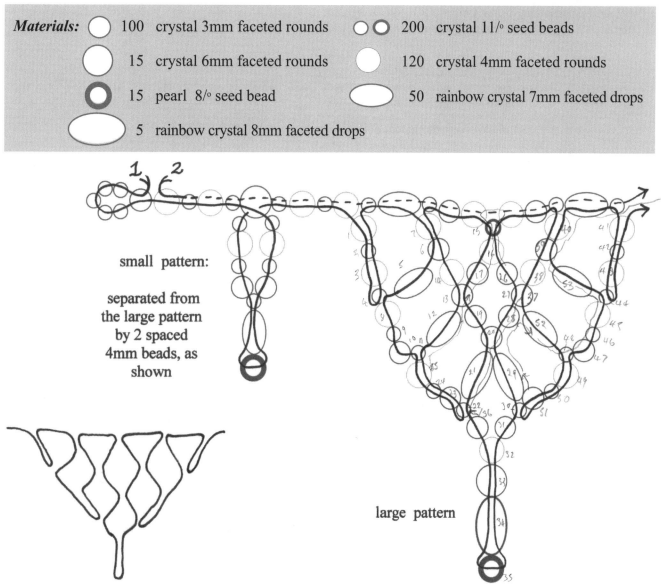

small pattern:

separated from the large pattern by 2 spaced 4mm beads, as shown

large pattern

BLUE CASCADE NECKLACE

Page 57

This 13-inch necklace is a bib of cascading sapphires; to lengthen it, add chain, or extra neckline pattern. The neckline is a 5 gold seed bead loop and 30 patterns of opal blue 11/° seed, 4mm cobalt blue, opal blue 11/° seed, each blue triplet separated by 2 gold seed beads. End with a 5 gold bead loop. Re-thread through the neckline, with a second thread, past the tenth 4mm round. From there, thread the first layer of hanging dangles, left to right. Add the lower layer, right to left, attaching at the top two beads of each previous dangle, forcing them forward as the thread goes *behind* then down through the connecting beads (lower dashed box). Follow the schematic, and note the closeup diagram on the next page.

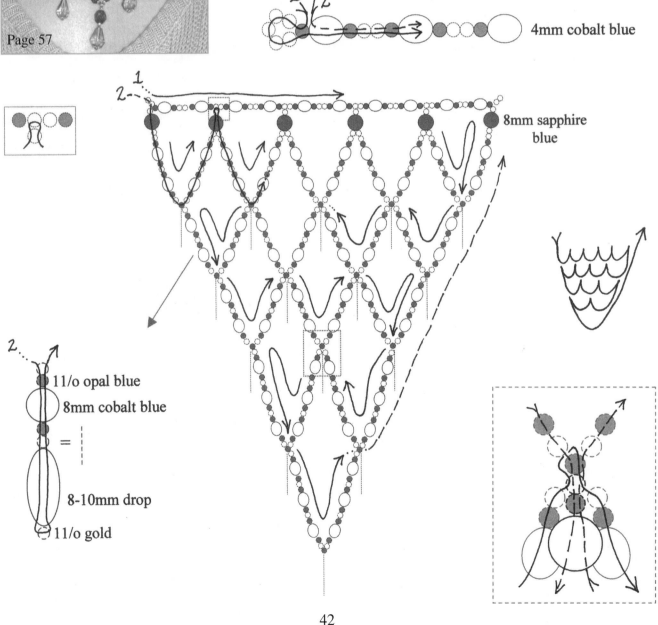

4mm cobalt blue

8mm sapphire blue

11/o opal blue

8mm cobalt blue

=

8-10mm drop

11/o gold

42

BLUE CASCADE NECKLACE

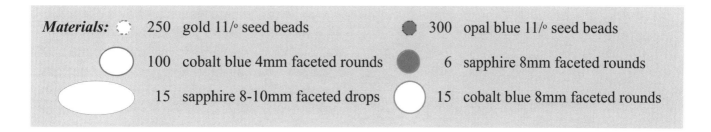

Materials:
- 250 gold 11/° seed beads
- 100 cobalt blue 4mm faceted rounds
- 15 sapphire 8-10mm faceted drops
- 300 opal blue 11/° seed beads
- 6 sapphire 8mm faceted rounds
- 15 cobalt blue 8mm faceted rounds

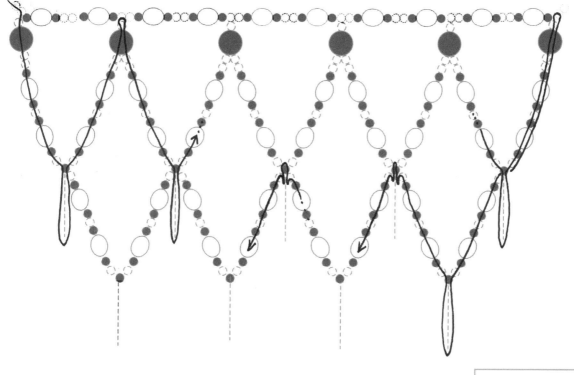

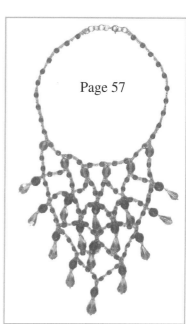

Page 57

LA CONDESSA'S NECKLACE

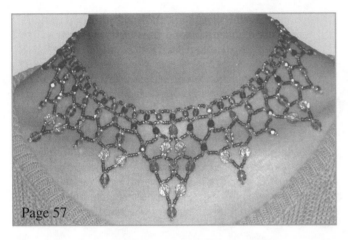

Page 57

A number of techniques makes this a challenging 14.5-inch necklace: a graduating network pattern that connects 4mm and 6mm faceted round beads and that is strung out along an arched neckline. Thread the ladder neckline (**a**) of 45 cobalt blue and lavender 4mm faceted round beads (start and end with cobalt blue), and add to it the netted pattern (**b**, **c**, **b** in reverse), beginning at the fifth 4mm cobalt blue neckline bead. The first netted triangle in **b** has topaz 4mm rounds, the second and fourth have bronze 4mm rounds and the third has a topaz and a ruby 4mm round, with cobalt, sapphire and cobalt blue 6mm rounds in the lower netting. Make sure the 11/° gold seed bead that has 4 threads going through it (see magnification below **c**) has an adequately large hole; test it first. Pattern **c** is actually composed, from left to right, of three netted triangles (small, larger/center, small): only two (small, larger/center) are shown. Do the third, smaller triangle like the first one and reverse the color scheme. The smaller triangles have a ruby and a garnet 4mm round, and repeat the cobalt, sapphire and cobalt blue 6mm rounds pattern in the lower netting. The large, central triangle has garnet 4mm rounds surrounding a 6mm faceted round pattern of alternating cobalt and sapphire blue (start and end with cobalt blue). Note that the method of attaching the netted pattern to the neckline changes, depending on whether the point of attachment is below a 4mm bead or in the middle of a lower link.

Materials:	400	gold 11/° seed beads		700	topaz silver-lined 11/° seed beads
	30	cobalt blue 4mm faceted rounds		30	lavender luster 4mm faceted rounds
	10	topaz luster jet 4mm faceted rounds		20	metallic gold 4mm faceted rounds
	10	garnet 4mm faceted rounds		4	ruby 4mm faceted rounds
	15	cobalt blue 6mm faceted rounds		15	sapphire blue 6mm faceted rounds

a

LA CONDESSA'S NECKLACE

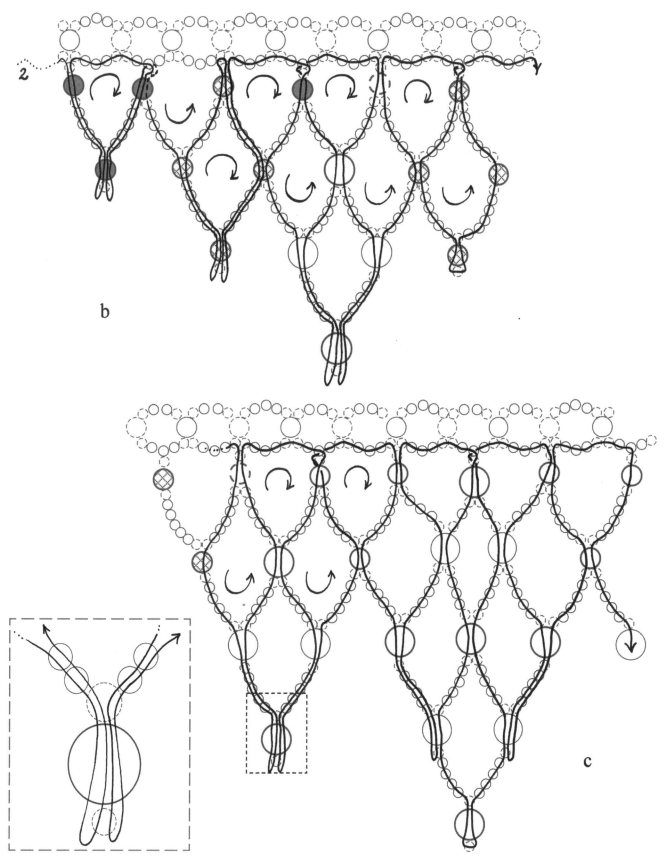

b

c

SUPERB SAPPHIRE NECKLACE

Page 58

Start this 13-inch necklace with a 7-bead silver seed bead loop, then add 14 rainbow sapphire 4mm beads spaced by single silver seed beads. Now add 21 ladder links of sapphire 4mm beads with neckline silver seed beads (**a**) and end with 14 silver spaced sapphire 4mm beads and a silver loop. Start and end the second thread where the first thread ends are, re-threading through the single neckline strand to the ladder and adding the second tier of 5 double concentric strands (**b**). Add the sapphire 6mm beads and then the sapphire 8mm beads for each set of concentric strands. Start the third thread at the thick lined bead to add the final large double concentric strands of sapphire 6mm beads (**c**).

Materials:

○	200	silver 11/° seed beads	○	140	rainbow sapphire 4mm faceted rounds
○	68	sapphire 6mm faceted rounds	○	15	sapphire 8mm faceted rounds

1

a

11/o seeds

2

4mm

b

8mm

6mm

SUPERB SAPPHIRE NECKLACE

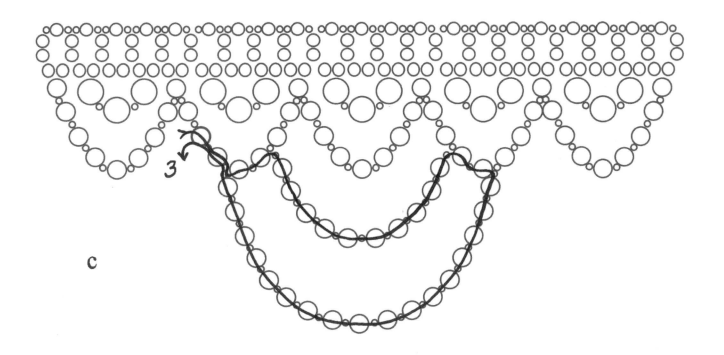

c

Page 58

NECKLACE AT TIFFANY'S

Page 58

No, I didn't see it there, but I couldn't resist the pun on the classic movie (if you're too young to get it, ask your parents). This truly royal looking creation is fairly easy to make. The loop is gold seed beads and the neckline pearl seeds with 4mm amethyst rounds. Make 14 teardrop patterns, alternating and ending with dropless patterns (15 in all) at both ends for a 14-inch necklace. These patterns have rainbow amethyst 5mm or 6mm rounds, gold seeds and an 8mm or 10mm faceted drop in the patterns with dangles. Attach the bottoms with trios of white pearl seeds, using a second thread (dashed line). Either of the earring patterns will match.

Materials: ○ 450 gold 10/° seed beads   ⬭ 200 opal pearl 11/° seed beads

⬭ 32 amethyst 4mm faceted rounds   ◯ 100 rb amethyst 5-6mm faceted rounds

⬭ 14 rainbow amethyst 8-10mm faceted drops

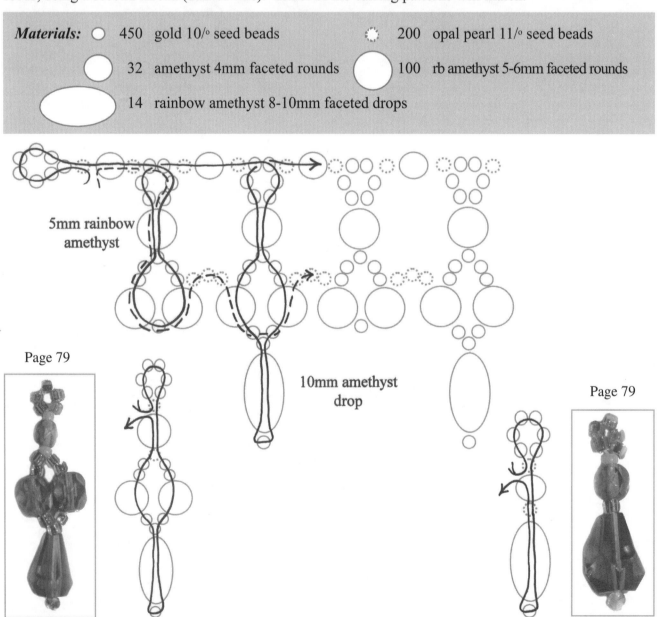

5mm rainbow amethyst

10mm amethyst drop

Page 79

Page 79

48

RUBY BEAUTY CHOKER

I spied this necklace in *Glamour* magazine adorning a model's neck - only hers was of red rubies set in gold with diamonds. Not having any rubies and diamonds on hand, I reached for the next best thing - my beads. The resulting 14-inch layered necklace of 41 repeating patterns, composed of 2 horizontal layers of beadwork, is a pretty glamorous mimic! Start by threading the gold and silver neckline with the 8mm ruby round layer and finish this layer as it was begun, with a gold loop. Use a new thread to add the second layer of 7mm by 6mm ruby faceted drops, 4mm jet faceted rounds and 6mm crystal faceted rounds. The netting effect is created by the shared jet round in each drop.

Page 59

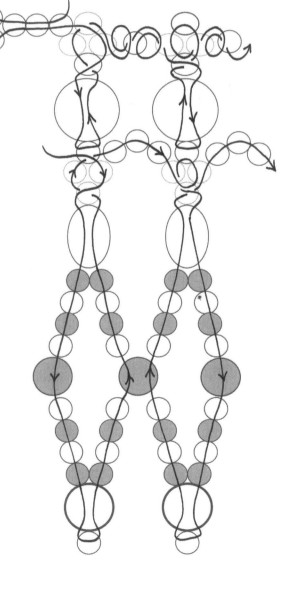

Materials:

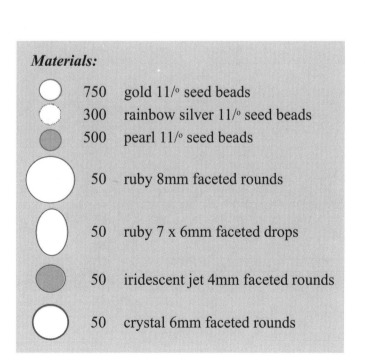

○	750	gold 11/° seed beads
◌	300	rainbow silver 11/° seed beads
●	500	pearl 11/° seed beads
◯	50	ruby 8mm faceted rounds
◯	50	ruby 7 x 6mm faceted drops
●	50	iridescent jet 4mm faceted rounds
◯	50	crystal 6mm faceted rounds

DIVA'S DELIGHT NECKLACE

Page 59

For the buxom bosomed madame who needs that special necklace for the opera, here it is. This 14-inch necklace is an elaboration of the Superb Sapphire Necklace (previous two pages); refer to its (**a**) and (**b**) diagrams for threading the ladder links and the second tier of double, now 7 concentric strands in this project. Start and end with a gold seed bead loop and 10 amethyst 4mm rounds spaced by gold seed beads; add 29 ladder links in the middle, using gold seed beads and 4mm beads of amethyst (top), rainbow finished lavender (the sides) and garnet (the 2 bottom beads).

With a second thread make 7 double concentric patterns, using gold spaced 6mm amethyst (sometimes rainbow finished amethysts for highlights) and 8mm amethyst faceted round beads, and 6mm gold core crystal faceted rounds at each apex of the double concentric patterns. Use a third thread to add a third tier of 3 single concentric strands and a fourth thread for the final tier of one large central concentric strand, following the diagrams below. Use gold spaced amethyst 6mm faceted rounds for these tiers and slightly lighter beads from a different batch to highlight the middle of the lowest arches. Check the lay of the necklace on the intended neck before permanently knotting the last 2 tiers; one or two beads might have to be added to each of the concentrics on these tiers to get the right angle of droop.

Materials:

○	250	gold 11/° seed beads	●	70	rainbow lavender 4mm faceted rounds
●	70	garnet 4mm faceted rounds	○	60	amethyst 4mm faceted rounds
○	10	gold core crystal 6mm faceted rounds	○	110	amethyst 6mm faceted rounds
○	25	amethyst 8mm faceted rounds			

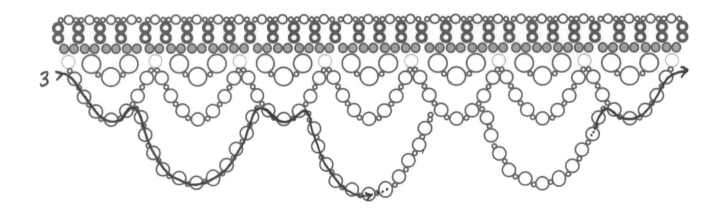

50

DIVA'S DELIGHT NECKLACE

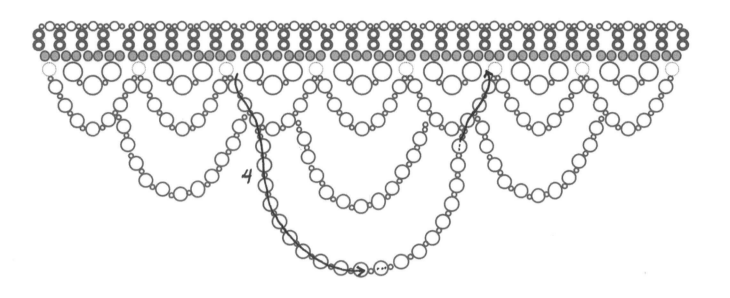

Page 59

Notes:

Chapter III: Bracelets

Bracelet design is restricted by both physical and aesthetic factors. Because a bracelet is subject to suddenly changing forces of gravity as a forearm moves up and down, beadwork designs are restricted to those that will not slide or twist too much. This doesn't leave much room for elaborate complexity when using large faceted beads. A big challenge is to create a clasp that is at least as heavy or heavier than any point along the rest of the bracelet. This is needed because gravity will often cause moving bracelets, especially around slender wrists, to end up with the heaviest point below the wrist. This is particularly true when the wrist is at rest horizontally and often means that the clasp is face up. Aesthetically, often a bracelet is worn as a matching accessory to a necklace, and is just a shortened sequence of the necklace; this can be done with projects such as the Modern Art Necklace and Glittering Choker. Conversely, any of the bracelet designs presented here can be lengthened into necklaces or chokers.

With three exceptions, the array of bracelet designs offered in this book are variations of chain sequences: a simple ladder sequence (Renaissance), a buttressed ladder sequence (Bauble), a chain sequence augmented by an overlain network on each chain (Bijou and Ribbon), and a ladder sequence where the point of connection changes to create a zigzag effect (Springtime and Grapevine).

The Diamond design is actually two looping strands connected in parallel, and buttressed or not. The Regal design is a simple netted band using beads of different sizes. Finally, the A la Fabergé design is a tube based on the quadrahelix or Dutch spiral beading pattern. The quadrahelix pattern is truly unique in that it is not, in the strict sense of the word, an interconnecting network of beads. Except for the initial and terminal circles of beads, the thread does not pass through a bead twice. Rather, the spiral of connecting loops are held together by tension and friction, although these spiral loops can also be connected via interconnecting beads.

By creating parallel connected chain sequences, one can widen several of the narrower bracelet designs into bands; look at the Victorian choker for pointers on how to proceed. Enjoy!

RENAISSANCE BRACELET

This 7.5-inch bracelet shows that even a simple pattern can produce a fancy piece. Start with a blue (B) dangle, then do 8 patterns of the bordered red (**R**) and blue faceted rounds as follows: BRBBRBBR. Note: the first and last patterns have modified endings for attaching to a dangle or loop. Finish with a loop that fits snugly over the dangle.

Page 60

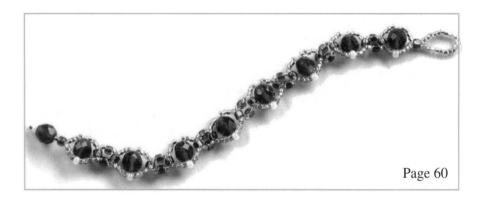

Page 60

Materials:
- ○ 200 gold 11/° seed beads
- ○ 35 topaz tinsel 6/° seed beads
- ○ 6 cobalt blue 8mm faceted rounds
- ○ 20 pearl 8/° seed beads
- ○ 3 ruby 8mm faceted rounds

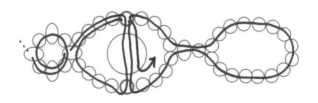

54

BAUBLE BRACELET

Flash this at some evening party! This 8-inch band bracelet is just a 7-inch ladder sequence of blue, red and green 4mm and 8mm faceted round beads. The edges of the 1-inch wide band are reinforced to keep it from collapsing. Do 24 of the vertical segments, then re-thread through the outer edges, adding a gold seed bead opposite to each 8mm bead, as shown. Add on a gold seed bead loop and a 6mm ruby red ball clasp at either end.

Page 60

Materials:
	300	gold 11/° seed beads
	50	pearl 8/° seed beads
	16	cobalt blue 4mm faceted rounds
	16	ruby red 4mm faceted rounds
	16	emerald green 4mm faceted rounds
	16	cobalt blue 8mm faceted rounds
	16	ruby red 8mm faceted rounds
	16	emerald green 8mm faceted rounds
	1	ruby red 6mm faceted round

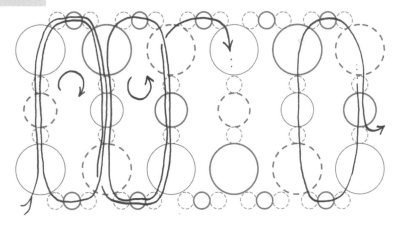

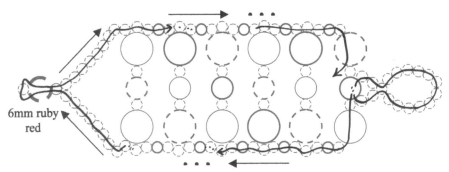

6mm ruby red

55

SPRINGTIME BRACELET

Page 60

Of course, by changing colors you can fit it to any season, any occasion. This delicate 8-inch bracelet is a zigzag ladder or chain sequence, using 11/° gold seed beads and 5 colors of 4mm faceted rounds: **j**onquil, **A**methyst, opal **p**ink, pale **i**ris, and iridescent **R**ose. Begin with a seed bead loop and do 18 4-petal flowers (**a**) in the following color sequence: **Rijp, Aijp, Rijp, Aijp, Ri**. Keep the work taut, ending with a clasp bead of any color.

Now re-thread back through the piece (**b**), keeping it taut throughout; the gold bead triplets between the flowers will be forced up. Make sure the triplets all pop up on the same side. Before knotting the end with the beginning thread, check that the loop is not too tight or loose for the clasp bead, and adjust accordingly.

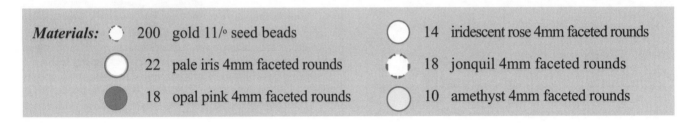

Materials:

○	200	gold 11/° seed beads
○	22	pale iris 4mm faceted rounds
●	18	opal pink 4mm faceted rounds
○	14	iridescent rose 4mm faceted rounds
⊙	18	jonquil 4mm faceted rounds
○	10	amethyst 4mm faceted rounds

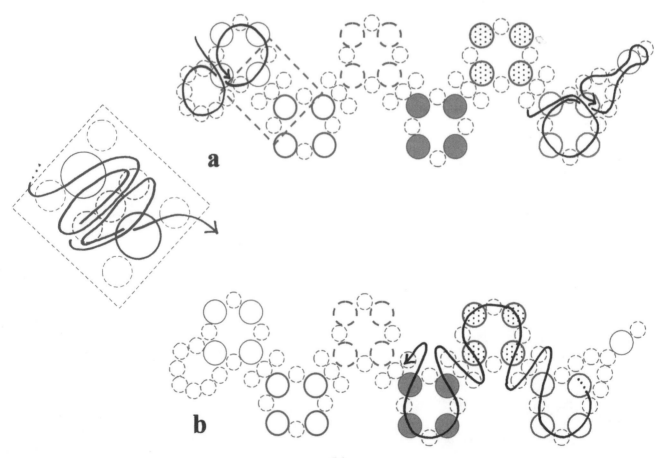

a

b

Page 42

Page 42

Page 44

Page 44

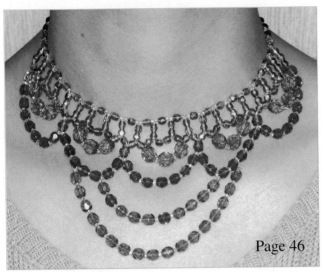

Page 46

Page 46

Page 48

Page 48

Page 49

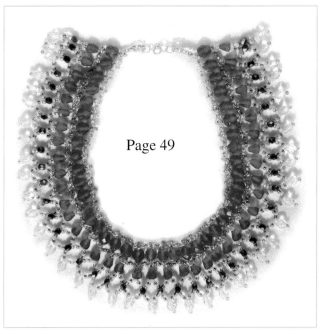

Page 49

Page 50

Page 50

59

Page 55

Page 54

Page 56

GRAPEVINE BRACELET

This is actually two zigzag ladder bracelets intertwined - how romantic! Create one 8.5-inch zigzag bracelet of gold 11/° seed beads and 10 quartets of iridescent black 4mm beads (**a**). Then create an equally long second bracelet of silver 11/° seed beads and light sapphire 4mm beads, but do not connect the ends yet). Intertwine the second bracelet with the first, lining up the quartets of 4mm beads in each bracelet opposite each other (**b**) and making sure not to introduce any twist into the second bracelet. At that point, close its juncture.

Page 77

Materials:

○ 200 gold 11/° seed beads
    200 silver 11/° seed beads

○   50 iridescent black 4mm faceted rounds
     50 light sapphire 4mm faceted rounds

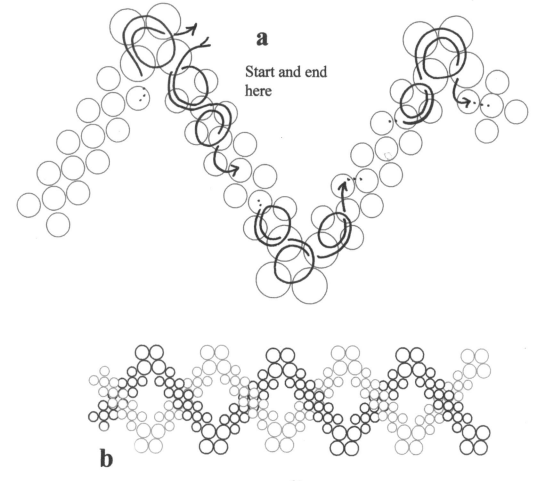

a

Start and end here

b

BIJOU BRACELET

Page 77

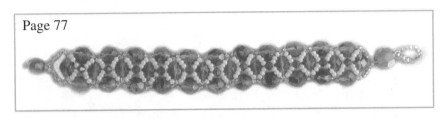

For the totally glam look, this is it. First make a dangle and a sequence of 11 chain link patterns (**a**). The chain links start and end with gold seed beads and a central topaz 8mm faceted round, followed by gold accented upper and lower topaz 8mm faceted rounds and central olivine 8mm faceted rounds. End with the loop of the clasp (**b**), using a 10mm bead (any color) to keep the weighted clasp below the wrist when worn. Then go back through the existing beadwork (**c**) to add on the latticework of 11/° pearl seed beads and 4mm red crystal rondelles, using 0 size Nymo thread; keep the work taut. *Variations:* 1) Wear it inside out! 2) Use 4 12/° pearl seed beads on the cross lengths for a better fit. 3) Lengthen it into a choker.

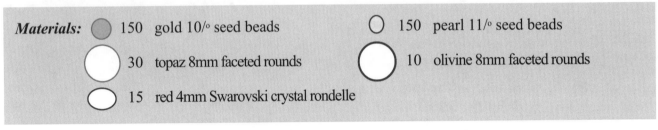

Materials: 150 gold 10/° seed beads   150 pearl 11/° seed beads

30 topaz 8mm faceted rounds   10 olivine 8mm faceted rounds

15 red 4mm Swarovski crystal rondelle

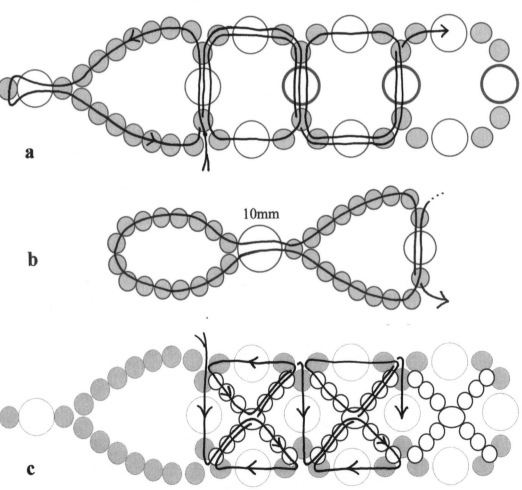

10mm

a

b

c

RIBBON BRACELET

Like the Bijou Bracelet, this is a chain with overlain work, but with a different effect: a spiral emerald ribbon rimmed with gold! Create 15 chain link patterns of emerald 10mm and jet 4mm faceted rounds interspersed with gold seed beads (**a**). Begin and end with a ball (another 10 mm bead) and loop clasp. Using the same thread, go back, overlaying the chain links with a spiral of gold and 8/° pearl seed beads (**b**) on one side; knot the thread ends together. *Variations:* 1) Wear it inside out! 2) turn the bracelet over & add a second spiral thread on the backside, spiraling in the same or opposite direction as the front; 3) lengthen it into a choker.

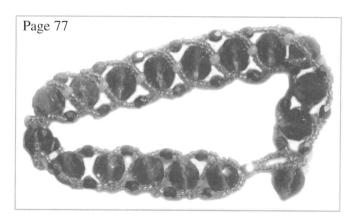

Page 77

Materials: ◯ 20 pearl 8/° seed beads

◯ 40 iridescent jet 4mm faceted rounds

⬤ ⬤ 400 gold 11/° seed beads

◯ 16 emerald 10mm faceted rounds

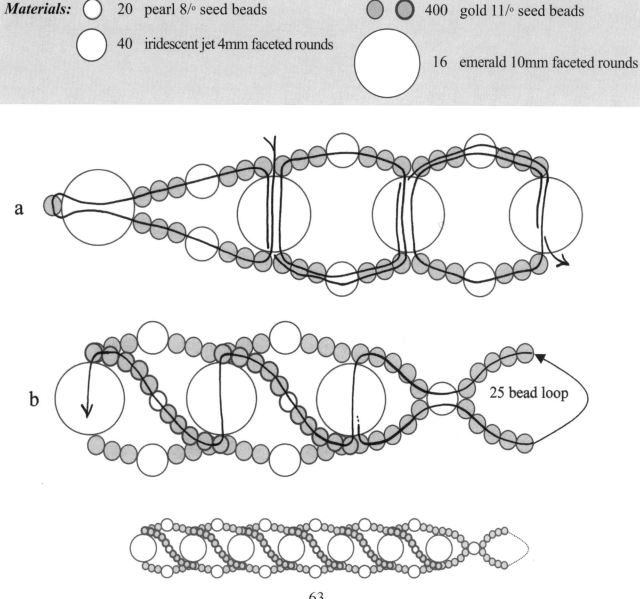

a

b

25 bead loop

63

DIAMOND BRACELET

Page 78

Diamonds in the pattern, not gemstone, sense - although you can mimic that, too, by replacing all the round faceted beads with Swarovski crystal. This 8-inch bracelet can be left at the first stage by doing only 7 diamond patterns (**a**), but the finished piece might twist a little when worn (bottom picture). Diamonds consist of olivine 6mm facetted round beads. They have gold and pearl accents and amber beads between them. Start and end at the *. To prevent twisting, continue threading to add crystal buttresses that connect the tips of the diamonds (**b**), but do 8 diamond patterns, which will compress when the buttresses are pulled taut. Note the bead sequence of the buttress between diamonds: 4 crystal and 1 gold seed bead, 4mm bead, 5 crystal and 1 gold seed bead. Also note that the sample pictured on the left has 9 diamond patterns with the crystal buttresses, which resulted in a rather long 9-inch bracelet.

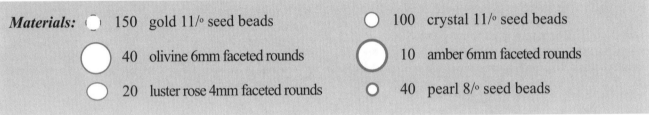

Materials:

○	150	gold 11/° seed beads	○	100 crystal 11/° seed beads
○	40	olivine 6mm faceted rounds	○	10 amber 6mm faceted rounds
○	20	luster rose 4mm faceted rounds	○	40 pearl 8/° seed beads

a

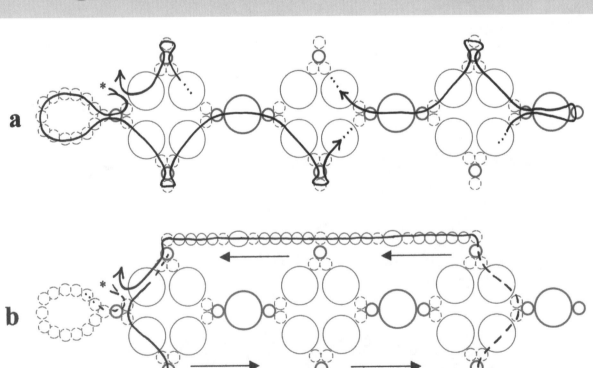

b

REGAL BRACELET

As one friend dubbed it, and so it is. This continuous beaded network can be stretched to slip over your hand. The length of 22 connected diagonals creates a stretched circumference of 9 inches. Every 6mm bead is connected by 3 seed beads (see highlighted seed beads in **a**) to the nearest faceted beads; all 4mm beads have 4 seed beads between them. The color sequence of the diagonals is: iridescent jet, amethyst, milky, amethyst, jet, amethyst, milky, amethyst. The amethyst diagonals have two central 6mm beads; the rest have four 4mm beads. Connect the end to the beginning (**b**) to make a continuous band.

Page 78

Materials:

○ ○	600	gold 11/° seed beads
○	12	iridescent jet 4mm faceted rounds
○	25	amethyst 4mm faceted rounds
○	25	milky white 4mm faceted rounds
○	12	jet black 4mm faceted rounds
○	25	amethyst 8mm faceted rounds

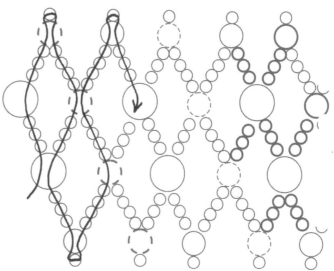

a

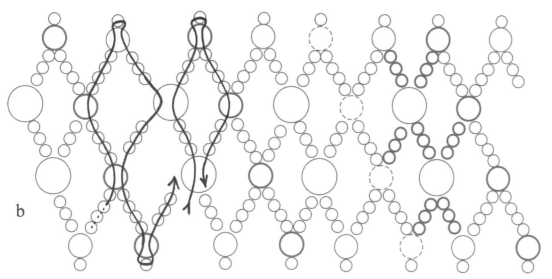

b

65

À LA FABERGÉ BRACELET

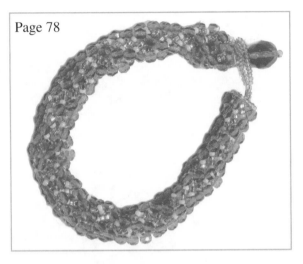

Page 78

This 8-inch tube bracelet is made with the Dutch Spiral (aka Quadrahelix) stitch, originally from Africa. Here, a spiral series of 4 tight loops slightly overlap, forcing the last bead of each loop to stand out; these form the 4 spiral ridges. Make a circle of 16 11/º transparent green beads and re-thread through them, pulling all **taut**, & knot. Initially, tape the 3-inch thread end to a chopstick put through the circle to hold the work. Add 5 beads: 4 seed (pearl, 2 gold, pearl) beads and one 4mm faceted round. Send the thread down through the top of the circle, pulling on the "up & down" parts of the thread to "snap" it into place between the 4th & 5th beads of the circle, and pull the loop tight. Keep **taut**. Repeat around the circle to make 4 loops. Make 4 more loops, this time securing each loop by "snapping" the thread between the 4th & 5th beads of the loop in the previous level above it.

Do about 200 loops (or 500 loops for a necklace). End with 4 loops of green seed beads, and re-thread through them, adding "filler" beads to create a circle. Fill the tube with a cotton cord to prevent collapse from wear. Add a 10mm faceted emerald green bead at one end and a 26 green seed bead loop at the other for a clasp (see Bijou Bracelet). *Variation:* You can achieve a similar effect by sending the thread through the bead on the right side of where it normally snaps into place.

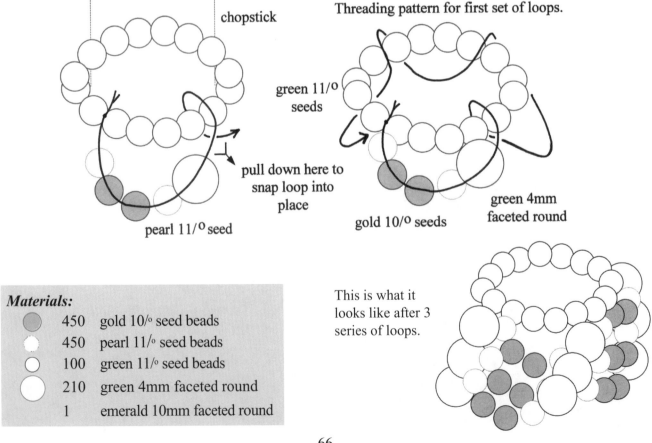

chopstick

Threading pattern for first set of loops.

green 11/º seeds

pull down here to snap loop into place

gold 10/º seeds

green 4mm faceted round

pearl 11/º seed

This is what it looks like after 3 series of loops.

Materials:

●	450	gold 10/º seed beads
○	450	pearl 11/º seed beads
○	100	green 11/º seed beads
○	210	green 4mm faceted round
	1	emerald 10mm faceted round

Notes:

Notes:

CHAPTER IV: EARRINGS & A RING

Since every hanging beadwork earring has to loop up to an earring finding, one can technically classify all earring designs as some form of modified loop. Ahhh, but what loops! The elaboration is seemingly endless. The ultimate restriction is weight and size - exactly how many grams are you willing to have tugging on your ear? How big is too big? For me, the answer is not more than the weight and size equivalent of eight 4mm or four 6mm faceted round beads, in addition to various connecting smaller beads, and this limits the designs presented here. But it shouldn't limit you: adapt the designs to your own creative urges and tolerance for weight.

The designs presented here are grouped into those that: 1) use a triplet or more of 4mm beads to achieve various effects (Empress, Gala, Bijou, Bell, Clover, Valentine, Tetra, Razzleberry, Blossom); 2) create a medallion effect (Bijou, Forget-Me-Not, Fleur de Lis, Medallion, Versatile Versailles); and 3) a single, eclectic design that creates a twisted rope of beads (À la Fabergé). Several match either necklace or bracelet designs in this book (Empress, À la Fabergé, and Bijou), and in fact, a few necklace designs have earrings designs accompanying them (Byzantine Necklace, and Necklace at Tiffany's). Others are great for particular holidays (Bell, Gala, Razzleberry, Valentine, and Clover).

Beaded earrings make great gifts: they're compact, can be given as a custom made accessory or for a particular occasion, and take relatively little time or resources to make. With the exception of Versatile Versailles, most of the designs require a 10-inch length of size E thread per earring. Once you've mastered a particular design, you'll find that you can make a pair of earrings in a half hour or less.

If you really like a particular earring design, you might want to create a matching necklace by linking several copies of the earring motif together. This is, in fact, what led me to create Eugenie's necklace from the Empress earring design. Comparing the earrings and necklace, you'll see that I modified the earring design for the necklace, using larger faceted beads to fit the grandeur of a larger piece. The same can be done with any of the designs.

I offer only one ring design here, but basically it is a springboard from which to exercise your own creativity. A daisy chain is the best way to make the circular band; what you attach to it can be derived from the many motifs offered in this book.

BRIDAL EARRINGS

Surprise! Not one but at least six designs in this section of the book can be used for the big day, using gold and pearl seed beads, and crystal faceted beads. Here are the diagrams for them. Go to the individual descriptions elsewhere in this book for detailed instructions on how to create them. The Fleur de Lis earrings match the Bridesmaid's Lace Necklace.

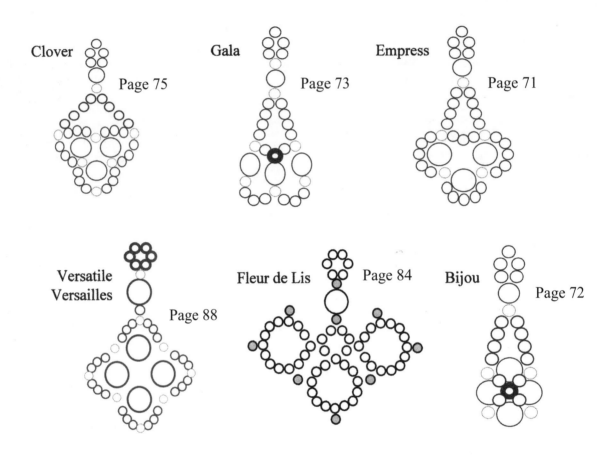

Clover — Page 75

Gala — Page 73

Empress — Page 71

Versatile Versailles — Page 88

Fleur de Lis — Page 84

Bijou — Page 72

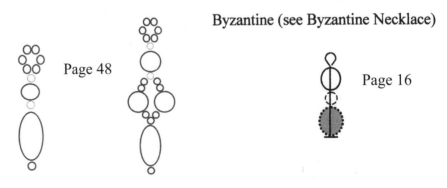

Tiffany's (see Necklace at Tiffany's) — Page 48

Byzantine (see Byzantine Necklace) — Page 16

EMPRESS EARRINGS

Make these elegant and easy earrings by first threading the amethyst top loop, then the first side of the amethyst and gold stem down to and through the 3 big bottom beads (amethyst 4mm faceted rounds). Follow by threading the amethyst and gold outer rim and the remaining side of the stem. Note that when the earring in the photograph was made, I added gold accents just below the finding loop and as the third bead in each sequence of five amethyst seed beads on the outer rim.

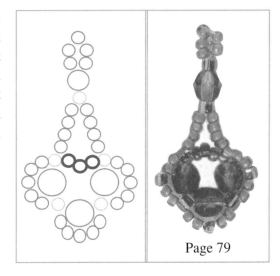

Page 79

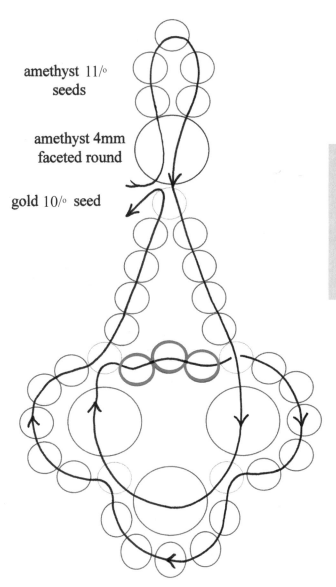

amethyst 11/° seeds

amethyst 4mm faceted round

gold 10/° seed

Materials:

○	60	amethyst core 11/° seed beads
○	20	gold 10/° seed beads
○	10	iridescent amethyst 11/° seed beads
○	10	amethyst 4mm faceted rounds

71

BIJOU EARRINGS

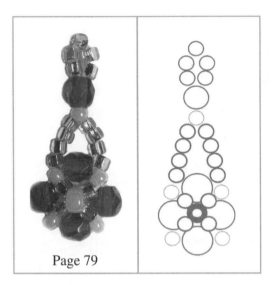

Page 79

Make these elegant drop earrings by first threading the gold top loop, then the first side of the ruby, pearl and gold stem down to and through the four big ruby 4 mm faceted round beads. Follow with the inner cross of gold and pearl beads and the remaining side of the stem. The thick rimmed bottom bead is an 8/° white pearl seed bead.

Materials:

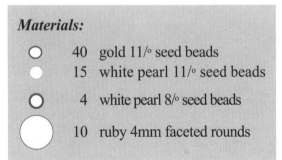

○	40	gold 11/° seed beads
○	15	white pearl 11/° seed beads
○	4	white pearl 8/° seed beads
○	10	ruby 4mm faceted rounds

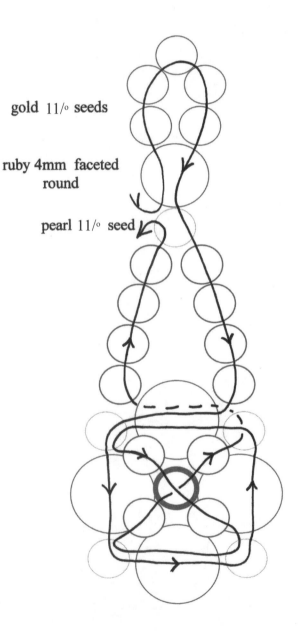

gold 11/° seeds

ruby 4mm faceted round

pearl 11/° seed

GALA EARRINGS

Make these fancy globular earrings by threading the right loop first (center & right cobalt blue 4mm beads) then the left loop. Re-thread the right loop, then up the stem and through the upper black loop, then down the other stem. Re-thread the left loop to the start and knot and hide the thread in the 8/° white pearl seed (thick rimmed) bead. The hole of the lowest gold (light gray line) bead must be able to fit 4 strands of thread.

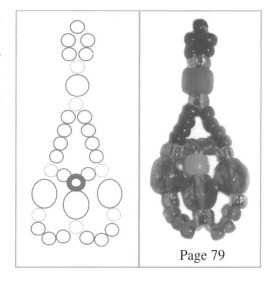

Page 79

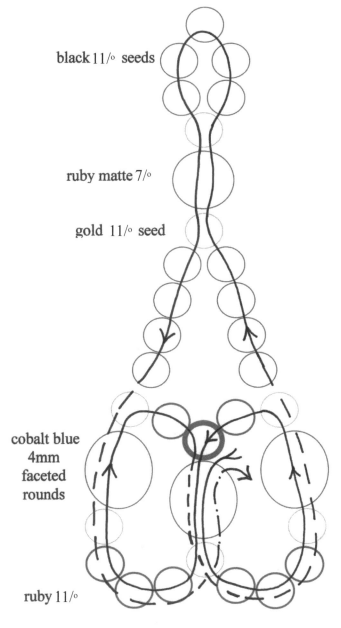

black 11/° seeds

ruby matte 7/°

gold 11/° seed

cobalt blue
4mm
faceted
rounds

ruby 11/°

Materials:

○	30	black 11/° seed beads
○	20	gold 11/° seed beads
○	20	ruby 11/° seed beads
◎	3	white pearl 8/° seed beads
○	3	ruby matte 7/° seed beads
○	8	cobalt blue 4mm faceted rounds

BELL EARRINGS

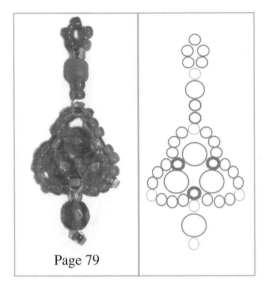

Page 79

I like to make these for the holidays. Thread the small top loop first, then the stem and the top, left red side of the bell. Add the green seed bead and 3 cobalt blue 4mm faceted round beads. Then thread the bottom left and right lobes of the bell, then the top, right side of the bell. Re-thread down through the bell as shown, add the gold seed bead and 4mm blue bead, then re-thread up through the bell and stem, back to the start. The lowest green seed bead must be able to accept 4 threads.

Materials:

○	20	garnet 11/° seed beads
○	10	gold 11/° seed beads
○	40	red 11/° seed beads
◉	10	green 11/° seed beads
○	4	ruby matte 7/° seed beads
○	10	cobalt blue 4mm faceted rounds

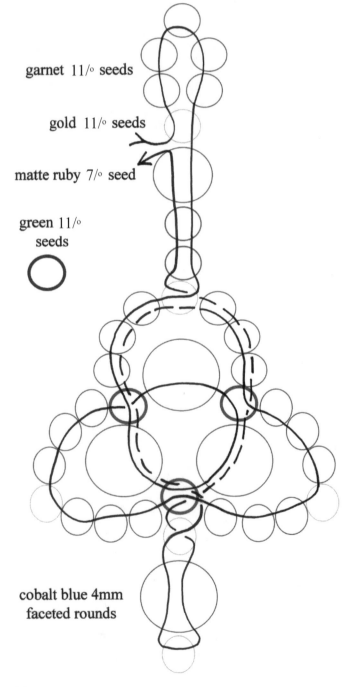

garnet 11/° seeds

gold 11/° seeds

matte ruby 7/° seed

green 11/° seeds

cobalt blue 4mm faceted rounds

CLOVER EARRINGS

A springtime earring! Start with the top green 4mm faceted round and thread the matte green top loop, then add a gold seed bead. Add the left half of the matte green top arch, then thread the loop of pearl seed beads and 3 green 4mm faceted rounds. Add the outer matte green and gold rim as shown, then the right half of the top arch. Re-thread through the gold seed bead to the start. If imperfections of the beads cause a lumpy profile, improve the curves of the outer rim by pushing the beads into place, then brushing the back of the rim with clear nail polish to hold the shape.

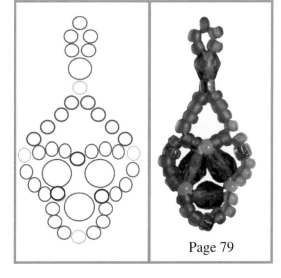

Page 79

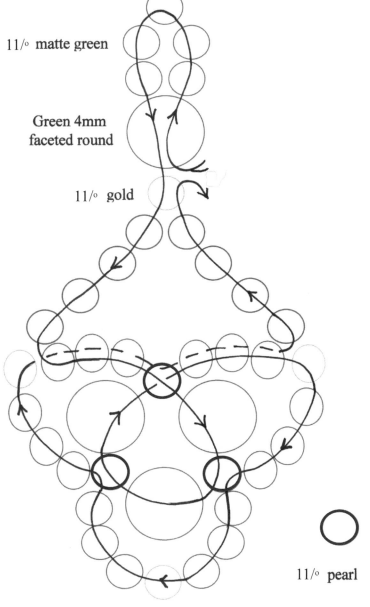

11/o matte green

Green 4mm
faceted round

11/o gold

11/o pearl

Materials:

○	70	matte green 11/o seed beads
○	10	gold 11/o seed beads
○	10	white pearl 11/o seed beads
○	10	green 4mm faceted rounds

VALENTINE EARRINGS

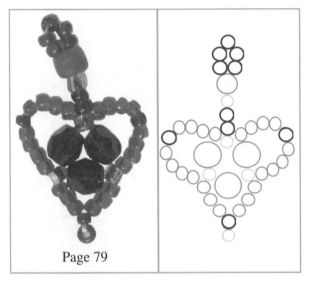

Page 79

A nice gift for your sweethearts on that special day. First thread the gold and garnet stem, then the ruby 7/° seed bead and garnet upper loop. Re-thread down the stem, adding the loop of a gold seed bead and 3 garnet 4mm faceted round beads. Then add the outer lobes of the heart back to the start and hide the knot in the 4mm bead. The hole of the first bead threaded must be able to fit 4 strands of thread. As with the Clover Earrings, you can improve the curves of the outer rim by pushing the beads into place, then brushing the back of the rim with clear nail polish to hold the shape. Note that the starting gold seed bead must be able to accept 4 threads.

Materials:

○	50	red 11/° seed beads
○	10	gold 11/° seed beads
○	20	garnet 11/° seed beads
○	4	ruby red matte 7/° seed beads
○	8	garnet 4mm faceted rounds

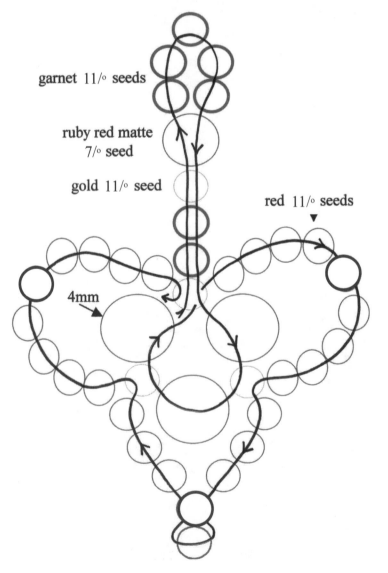

garnet 11/° seeds

ruby red matte 7/° seed

gold 11/° seed

red 11/° seeds

4mm

Page 61

Page 62

Page 63

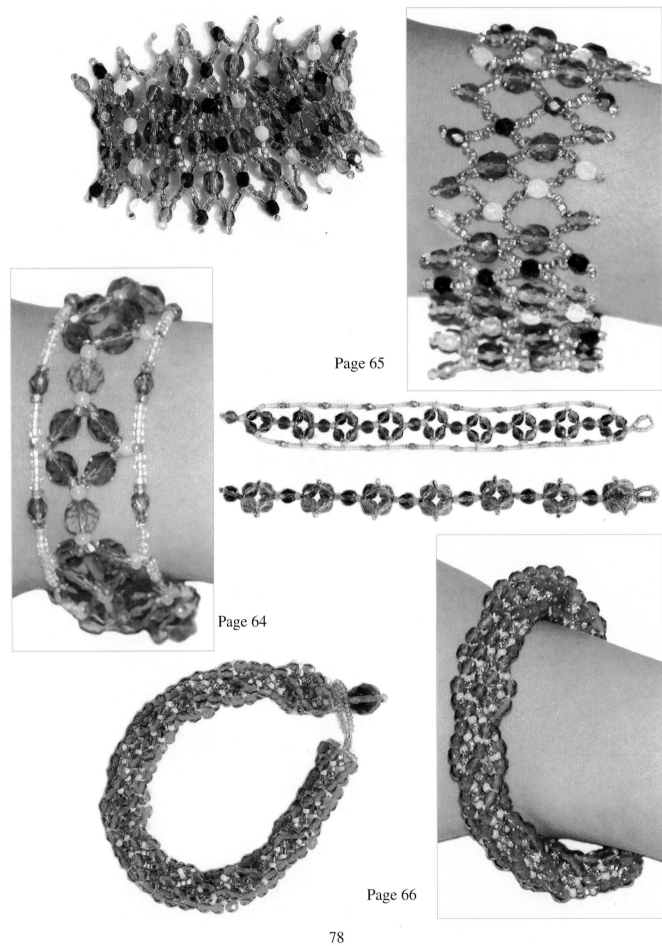

Page 65

Page 64

Page 66

78

Page 48

Page 71

Page 72

Page 73

Page 74

Page 75

Page 76

Page 81

Page 82

Page 83

Page 84

Page 85

Page 86

Page 87

Page 92

TETRA EARRINGS

Make these 3 dimensional earrings by first threading the green, topaz and silver seed bead stem. Add the central loop of silver seed beads and 3 green 4mm faceted round beads and then the outer topaz rim. Pull the rim taut, forcing the 3 big beads to form a tetrahedron pointing out from the page towards you. Then re-thread up the stem to the start; knot and trim.

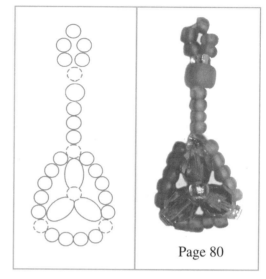

Page 80

matte topaz 11/° seeds

green '7/° seed

silver 11/° seed

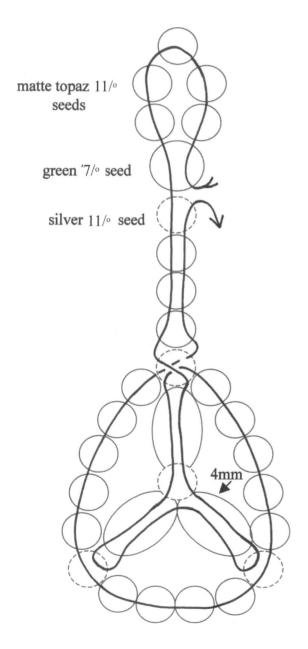

4mm

Materials:

○	50	matte topaz 11/° seed beads
◌	10	silver 11/° seed beads
◯	4	matte green 7/° seed beads
⬭	8	green 4mm faceted rounds

FORGET-ME-NOT EARRINGS

Page 80

And your friends won't, once you present them with a pair of these easy-to-make but memorable earrings. First create a curving ladder pattern of 7 light sapphire 4mm round faceted beads, with gold and blue seed beads interspersed. Then thread the blue and gold halter and top loop. Connect the halter to the curved ladder and go back to the start to knot and end the earring.

Materials:

○	25	tinsel blue 11/° seed beads
⬭	80	gold 11/° seed beads
◯	16	lt sapphire 4mm faceted rounds

gold 11/° seeds

blue tinsel 11/° seed

4mm

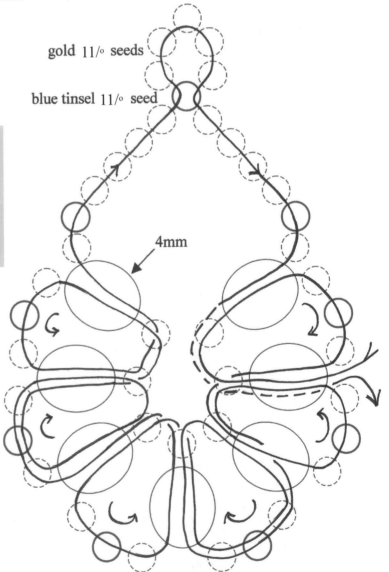

BLOSSOM EARRINGS

These superficially match the blossom necklace, but the structure is quite different. Six 4mm faceted round beads radiate from a central circular network (**a**) that is pushed out by a periphery pulled taut, as in the Tetra Earrings. Start by threading a pearl 8/° seed bead and the gold top loop and stem. Then add the first amethyst 4mm faceted round, followed by the central circle of gold seed beads. Add 5 more amethyst 4mm beads and their gold accents around the central circle. Then thread the outer rim and pull it taut to push out the interior beadwork. End with a central 4mm bead (**b**). Re-thread back up to the starting point, knot the thread ends and hide the knot in the pearl seed bead.

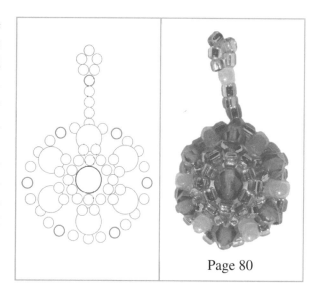

Page 80

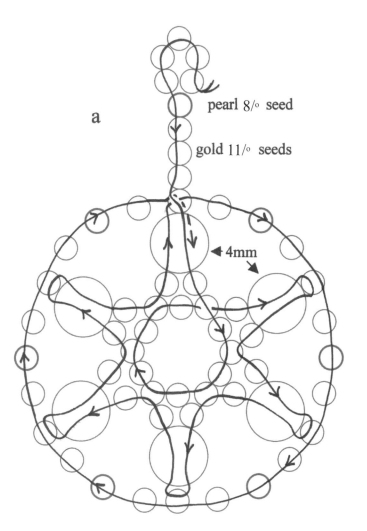

a

pearl 8/° seed

gold 11/° seeds

◀ 4mm

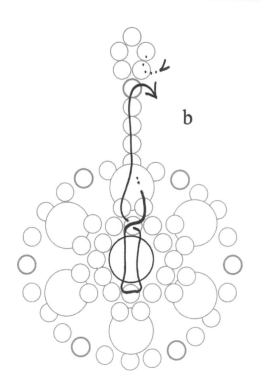

b

Materials:

○	120	gold 11/° seed beads
○	16	white pearl 8/° seed beads
⃝	14	amethyst 4mm faceted rounds

83

FLEUR DE LIS EARRINGS

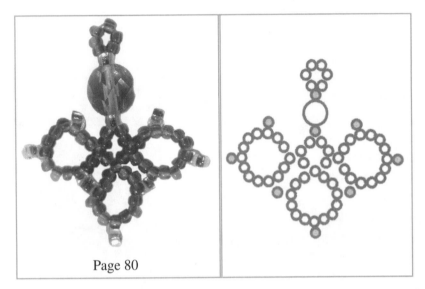

Page 80

I've sold many of these elegant, simple earrings to a local boutique, where they complement everything. Now you can make them yourself! These also complement the tatted lace Bridesmaid's Necklace in style. Start by threading the silver and amethyst top loop, add the sapphire 6mm faceted round and thread the loops of the fleur de lis as shown. Keep the work taut, and thread twice through the single beads that are looped to the frame. Pull taut when tying the ends together, and send the remaining ends down through the big bead, pulling the knot inside.

Trim the thread ends. Use a pen or other point to "shape" the 3 loops by pushing the beads into appropriate positions. Brush the back of the beadwork with nail polish to hold the shape.

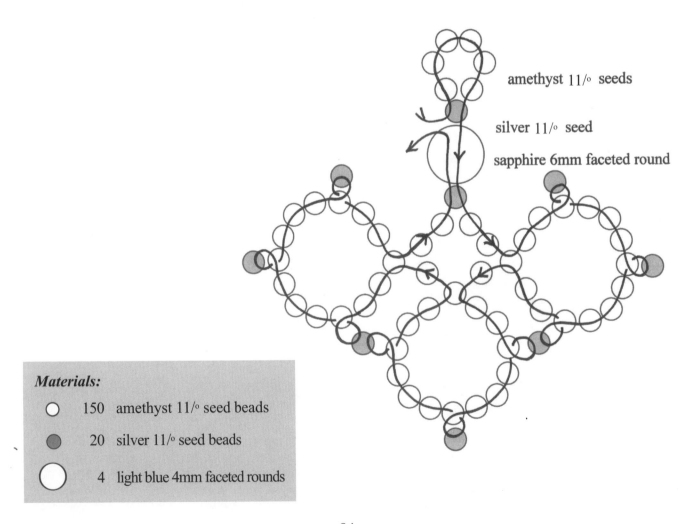

amethyst 11/° seeds

silver 11/° seed

sapphire 6mm faceted round

Materials:

○   150   amethyst 11/° seed beads

●   20   silver 11/° seed beads

○   4   light blue 4mm faceted rounds

RUBY EARRINGS

This is a good general festive design, straightforward and easy to execute. Start by threading the inner circle of gold seed beads, then add the 5 petals of 4mm ruby faceted rounds and ruby seed beads as shown. Finally add the central faceted bead, and re-thread up to form the top halter and loop (gold and ruby seed beads).

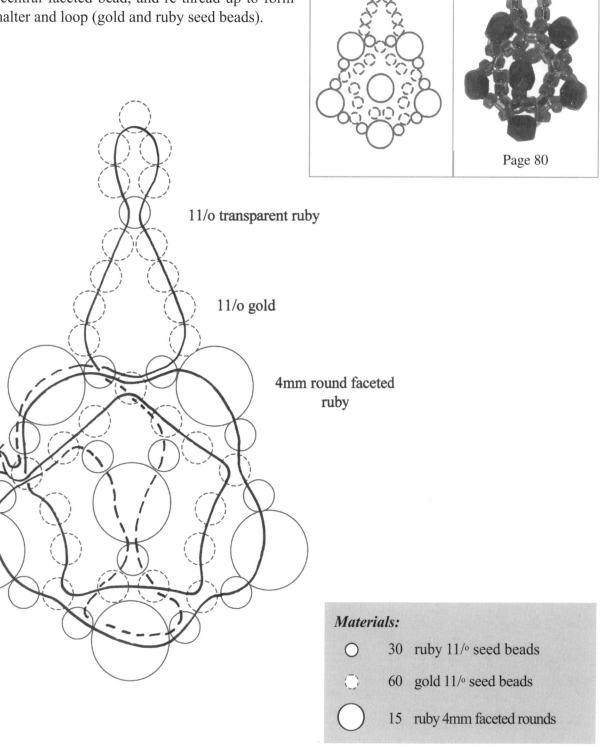

Page 80

11/o transparent ruby

11/o gold

4mm round faceted ruby

Materials:

○   30   ruby 11/o seed beads

○   60   gold 11/o seed beads

○   15   ruby 4mm faceted rounds

85

RAZZLEBERRY EARRINGS

Page 80

This is just a circular ladder of small (11/° gold) and big (4mm ruby faceted round) beads, reinforced through the middle with big beads (dashed beads in **f**). Study the threading diagrams carefully before beginning. Start with the gold loop and stem, then the ladder (**a-d** shows each face as you turn the piece 90°). There are four sets of 2 vertical beads in the ladder and each set is shown twice in diagrams **a-d**; that is, the beads shown on the right in diagram **a** are also shown on the left in diagram **b**. Connect the beginning with the end (diagram **d**), creating a circle (**e**, bottom view). Then thread the reinforcing beads through the chain (**f**: all 4 faces are shown simultaneously by giving 2 views of each vertical pair of big beads, thus the 2nd and 3rd vertical pairs in the diagram are the *same* beads, as are the 4th and 5th, etc.). Finally, re-thread back up to and through the top bead *opposite* the top bead connected to the stem, and re-thread up the stem to the beginning and knot (**g**).

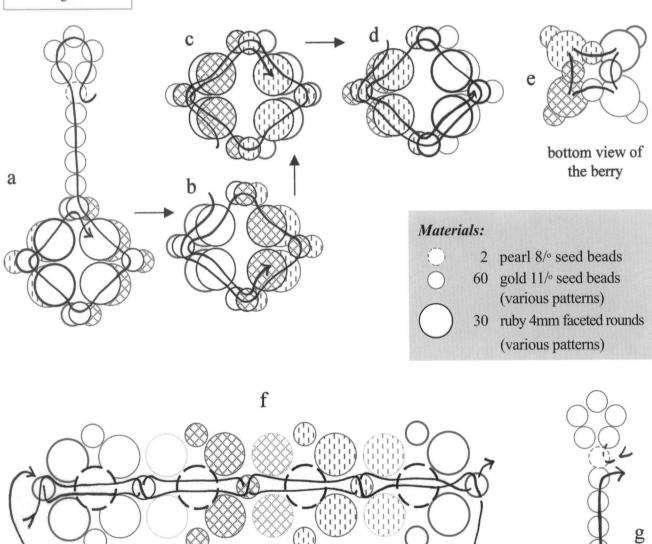

bottom view of
the berry

Materials:

⦾	2	pearl 8/° seed beads
○	60	gold 11/° seed beads (various patterns)
◯	30	ruby 4mm faceted rounds (various patterns)

MEDALLION EARRINGS

You can make one to hang from a simple chain to dress up any outfit, or make two for an elaborate pair of earrings – that's what Mom wanted. Start in the center and work out, creating the concentric layers of the medallion and the top loop (see diagrams); re-thread back to the center and knot the two ends. The 14 dark green beads around the center bead will tighten up, hugging the center, as you finish. Keep the work taut.

Page 80

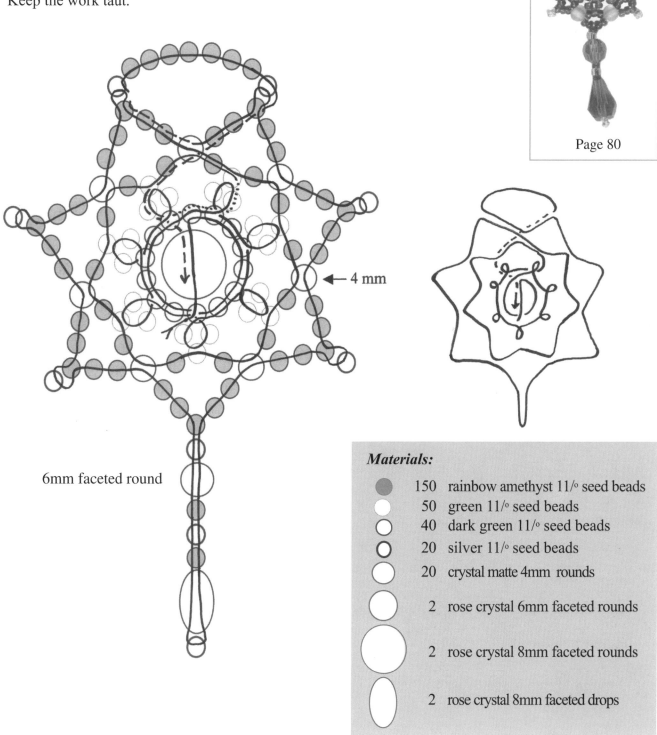

← 4 mm

6mm faceted round

Materials:

●	150	rainbow amethyst 11/° seed beads
○	50	green 11/° seed beads
○	40	dark green 11/° seed beads
○	20	silver 11/° seed beads
○	20	crystal matte 4mm rounds
○	2	rose crystal 6mm faceted rounds
○	2	rose crystal 8mm faceted rounds
○	2	rose crystal 8mm faceted drops

Versatile Versaille Earrings

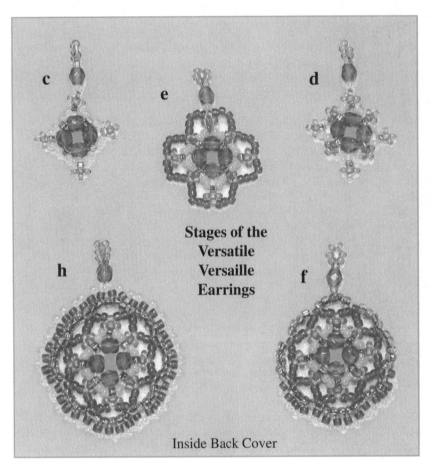

Stages of the
Versatile
Versaille
Earrings

Inside Back Cover

Capturing the Old World élegance with seed and 4mm and 6mm faceted round beads, this versatile design ranges from simple to elaborate, depending on what stage you stop adding to it. To end, always re-thread to the beginning and knot. Try different color combinations, substituting purple for the green or using olive and sea green instead of green and dark green.

Materials:

85	green 11/° seed beads
160	dark green 11/° seed beads
100	gold tinsel 10/° seed beads
120	white pearl 11/° seed beads
12	green 4mm faceted rounds

The first stage (**a**) can be slightly modified (**b**) to create elegant dangling diamonds.

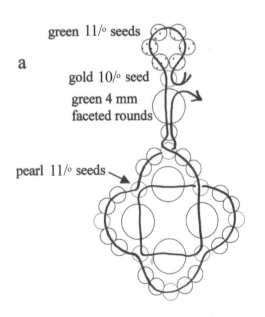

green 11/° seeds

gold 10/° seed

green 4 mm
faceted rounds

pearl 11/° seeds

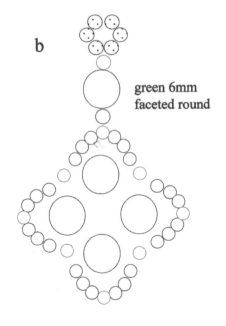

green 6mm
faceted round

88

Versatile Versaille Earrings

At the second stage, a partial (**c**) or full fringe (**d**) can be added to the diamonds. Wax the fringe thread to stiffen the resulting fringe.

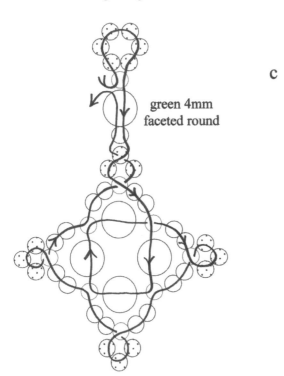

c

green 4mm
faceted round

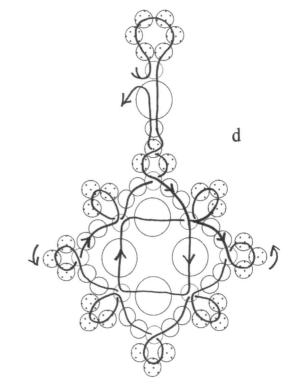

d

At the third stage (**e**), another fringe or layer is

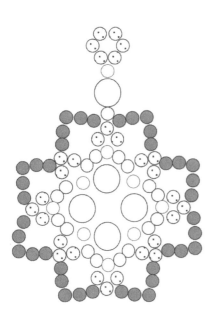

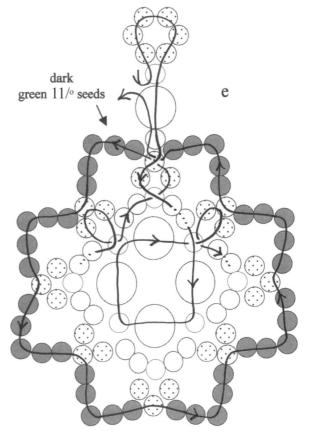

dark
green 11/o seeds

e

Versatile Versaille Earrings (cont.)

At the fourth stage (**f**), two further layers are added, as well as an outer, lower fringe.

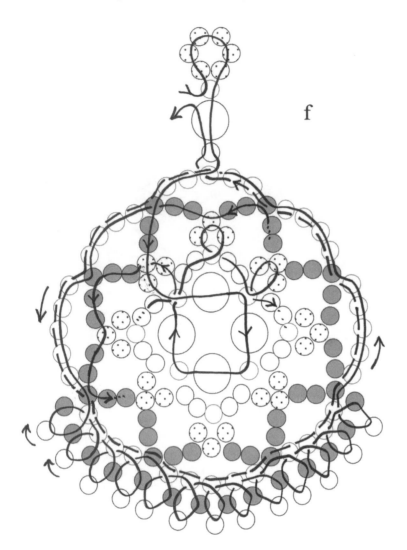

f

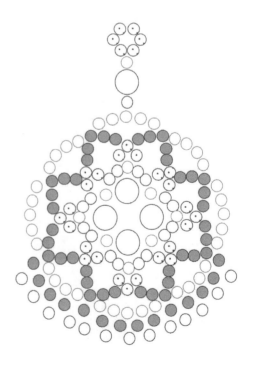

Versatile Versaille Earrings (cont.)

Alternatively, the entire outer rim can be fringed, working clockwise, for the final stage (**g, h**).

Fringe ends here …

And starts here …

g

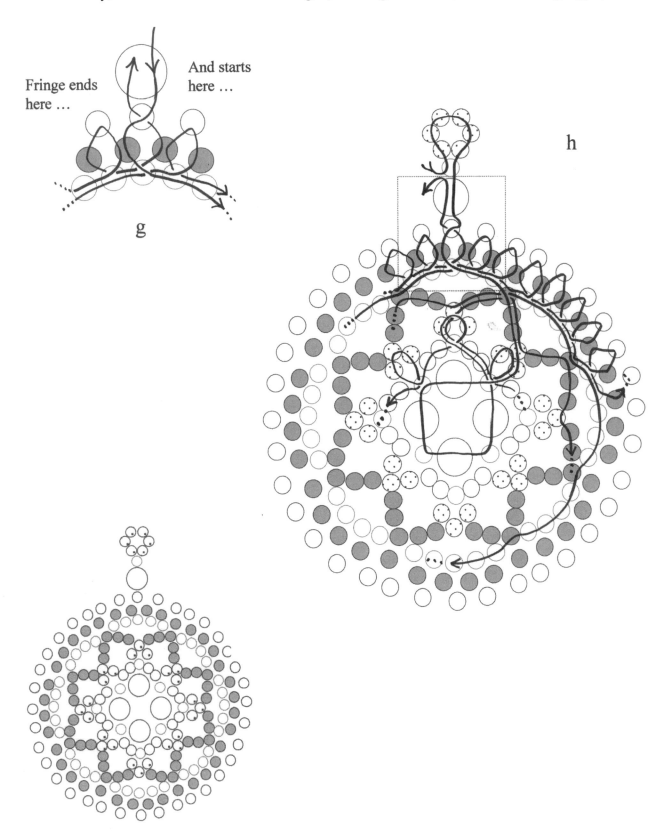

h

À LA FABERGÉ EARRINGS

Page 80

Spiraling loops of green beads threaded along a central line of gold beads create this twisted rope pattern. Use Nymo size 0 thread. To start, thread a circle of 4 gold beads and 3 green beads, re-threading through the golds, as shown. *Add one gold bead and 3 green beads to the thread. Starting between the first and second gold beads of the circle, re-thread forward through the remaining 3 golds *and* the latest gold bead added (4 in all). Pull taut. You now have 2 loops attached to the central gold line. Keep repeating from the *, adding a gold and 3 green beads (the loop) to the gold line (starting one gold bead forward each time), until you have done 36 loops or about a 2 1/4" length of this stitch.

Now go to the beginning between the first and second gold bead and re-thread backward through the first gold bead to the starting point. Pull the work taut so as to create a large loop of twisted rope. Add a loop of 6 gold beads, knot and hide the ends. This pattern goes well with the Fabergé bracelet and necklace. *Variations:* alternate gold beads with white pearl ones; use silver & red for candy cane earrings!

Materials:

◯　100　gold 10/° seed beads

●　400　green 11/° seed beads

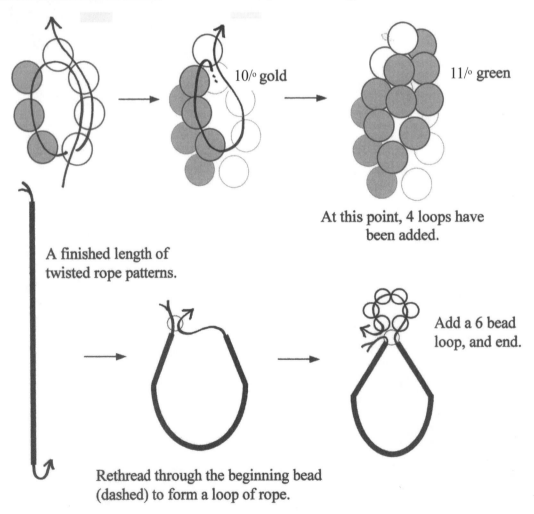

10/° gold

11/° green

At this point, 4 loops have been added.

A finished length of twisted rope patterns.

Rethread through the beginning bead (dashed) to form a loop of rope.

Add a 6 bead loop, and end.

BIJOU RING

This is just the beginning of the different design motifs you can use from this book to come up with your own, original ring. Start with the centerpiece, as shown in the diagram and add the 11 daisy chain sequence. Connect the end of the chain to the other side of the centerpiece to form a 15mm diameter ring; for larger rings, add more daisies. Use Swarovski crystals!

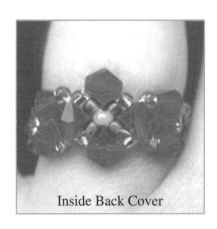

Inside Back Cover

Materials:

○	150	gold 11/° seed beads
○	20	pearl 11/° seed beads
○	25	dark green 11/° seed beads
⬭	20	ruby 4mm faceted rounds

Start & end here

. . 10 . . 11   Counting daisies: 1 . . . 2 . . . 3 . . . 4 . .

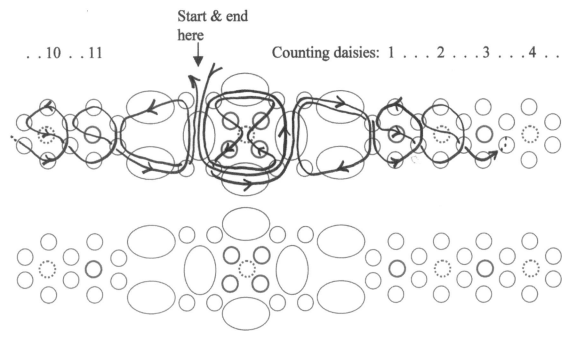

93

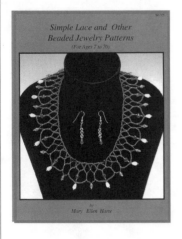

SIMPLE LACE AND OTHER BEADED JEWELRY PATTERNS:
For Ages 7 To 70
by Mary Ellen Harte

This is the first seed bead workbook, written with beaders of all ages in mind, to supply large, clear, graphic illustrations as well as instructions on how to thread many popular jewelry patterns. This presentation provides the framework for creating attractive and colorful necklaces, rings, bracelets, earrings and napkin holders. The patterns come from diverse cultures throughout the world, many of which were collected by the author during her travels. This is a wonderful new book for beaders of all ages and skills!

THE BEADING OF MY HEART:
52 Loom Beading Projects
by Mary L. Thompson

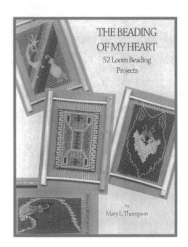

Learn Loom Beading the Easy Way with the Mini-Frame Loom!
Anyone wanting to learn Loom Beading can pick up this book, buy supplies with confidence, build a simple frame loom and complete a project. All aspects of beginning bead looming are covered. The patterns are beautiful, ranging broadly from Navajo rug designs to Orcas, and they will charm beadworkers of all skill levels. All the patterns can be used on larger looms. There are step by step instructions and every pattern has a color code, bead count, and color photo. Beading graph paper is also included. This book has it all. 116 fun-filled pages. A book you won't want to miss!

TRADITIONAL INDIAN CRAFTS
by Monte Smith

This book includes complete, illustrated instructions on all the basics of Leather, Bone and Feather crafts of the American Indian. Projects include: Bear Claw Necklace, Imitation Bone Hairpipe Breastplate, Sioux Dancing Choker, Quilled Medicine Wheels, Dancing Bell Set, Feathered Dance Whistle, the beautiful Double-Trailer Warbonnet and much more. In addition, craft techniques described include quill wrapping, shaping feathers, how to size projects, using imitation sinew, how to antique bone, obtaining a "finished" look and hints on personalizing craft projects. Designed so even beginners can create authentic Indian crafts with ease!

A TREASURY OF BEADED JEWELRY:
Bead Stringing Patterns For All Ages
by Mary Ellen Harte

Dazzled by the beautiful beadwork of native peoples near and far? This culturally rich mix of seed bead patterns will satisfy the young beginner, the advanced crafter and the holiday giftmaker. This book makes learning to create beautiful necklaces, chokers, bracelets, belts, pouches and headbands a snap. From simple Y necklaces to elaborate Romanian collars and original designs by the author, each pattern is graphically diagrammed for easy use and is also accompanied by simple and clear written instructions. These are stringing patterns and require no elaborate stitching techniques. The projects result in lovely, fashionable pieces which you and your friends will be proud to wear on any occasion. A great new release you won't want to miss!

HEMP MASTERS GETTING KNOTTY:
Ancient Hippie Secrets for Knotting Hip Hemp Jewelry
by Max Lunger

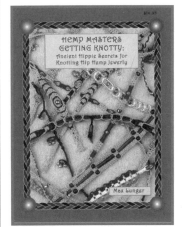

Max does it again! This is a simple, easy to follow, instructional guide to creating outstanding hemp jewelry. It features the use of colored hemp and 22 fantastic patterns. With a little hippie humor, this guide will keep you smiling as you learn. There are an abundance of illustrations and photographs to complement the clear, complete instructions. The projects include chokers, necklaces, anklets, a belly chain with bells, bracelets and a belt (it is gorgeous). Finally there are four patriotic projects in red, white and blue, including an American flag tied with alternating square knots, a USA armband (learn to tie the letters of the alphabet), a lacy bracelet and a proud American rear view mirror charm.

BEADED TREASURE PURSES:
Tubular Brick Stitch Designs
by Deon DeLange

Let the Master of Brick Stitch, teach you an entirely new and easy way to make these very popular small beaded necklace purses. Deon's designs are one of her hallmarks and the ones in this book make incredibly beautiful purses using either delica beads or size 11 seed beads. The book introduces Tubular Brick Stitch techniques, which are much easier to use than the more commonly taught techniques. The book is fully illustrated with easy-to-follow instructions and lots of photographs. Each design is graphed. Included are many ideas for trimming the edges of a purse, as well as a variety of necklace strap suggestions. The exciting, new Freeform beading stitch is also introduced.

EAGLE'S VIEW PUBLISHING BEST SELLERS

❏	**The Technique of Porcupine Quill Decoration** by W. Orchard	B00/01	$9.95
❏	**Technique of North American Indian Beadwork** by Monte Smith	B00/02	$13.95
❏	**Techniques of Beading Earrings** by Deon DeLange	B00/03	$9.95
❏	**More Techniques of Beading Earrings** by Deon DeLange	B00/04	$9.95
❏	**New Adventures in Beading Earrings** by Laura Reid	B00/07	$9.95
❏	**Beads and Beadwork of the American Indian** by Orchard	B00/08	$16.95
❏	**The Beading of My Heart: 52 Loom Beading** by Mary Thompson	B00/09	$15.25
❏	**Traditional Indian Crafts** by Monte Smith	B00/10	$12.95
❏	**Traditional Indian Bead & Leather Crafts** by Smith/VanSickle	B00/11	$12.95
❏	**Adventures in Creating Earrings** by Laura Reid	B00/14	$9.95
❏	**A Quillwork Companion** by Jean Heinbuch	B00/17	$14.95
❏	**Making Indian Bows & Arrows...The Old Way** by D. Spotted Eagle	B00/18	$12.95
❏	**A Beadwork Companion** by Jean Heinbuch	B00/22	$12.95
❏	**Beads and Cabochons** by Patricia Lyman	B00/23	$10.95
❏	**Earring Designs by Sig** by Sigrid Wynne-Evans	B00/24	$10.95
❏	**Voices of Native America** by Douglas Spotted Eagle	B00/29	$17.95
❏	**Craft Cord Corral** by Janice S. Ackerman	B00/30	$8.95
❏	**Hemp Masters** by Max Lunger	B00/31	$13.95
❏	**Plains Indian and Mountain Man Crafts I** by C Overstreet	B00/34	$13.95
❏	**Beaded Images: Intricate Beaded Jewelry** by Barbara Elbe	B00/35	$10.95
❏	**Simple Lace & Other Beaded Jewelry Patterns** by M. E. Harte	B00/41	$7.95
❏	**Beaded Treasure Purses** by Deon DeLange	B00/42	$10.95
❏	**The Art of Simulating Eagle Feathers** by Gutierrez	B00/43	$9.95
❏	**A Treasury of Beaded Jewelry** by Mary Ellen Harte	B00/44	$8.95
❏	**Hemp Masters - Getting Knotty** by Max Lunger	B00/45	$14.95
❏	**Beading Beautiful Costume Jewelry** by Mary Ellen Harte	B00/46	$17.95
❏	**Eagle's View Publishing Catalog of Books**	B00/99	$4.00

At your local bookstore or use this handy form for ordering:

EAGLE'S VIEW PUBLISHING READERS SERVICE, DEPT BBCJ
6756 North Fork Road - Liberty, Utah 84310

Please send me the above title(s). I am enclosing $_____ (Please add $6.50 per order to cover shipping and handling.) Send check or money order - no cash or C.O.D.s please.

Ms./Mrs./Mr. _____

Address _____

City/State/Zip Code _____

Prices and availability subject to change without notice. Please allow three to four weeks for delivery.

BBCJ-03/05